Gumboot Guys

02 03 04 05 27 26 25 24

Caitlin Press Inc.
3375 Ponderosa Way
Qualicum Beach, BC V9K 2J8
www.caitlinpress.com

Text design, map (page 8) and cover design by Vici Johnstone
Cover image courtesy Rob Pettigrew
Title page and back cover illustration by Bill Smith
Printed in Canada

Caitlin Press Inc. acknowledges financial support from the Government of Canada and the Canada Council for the Arts, and the Province of British Columbia through the British Columbia Arts Council and the Book Publisher's Tax Credit.

Library and Archives Canada Cataloguing in Publication

Gumboot guys : nautical adventures on British Columbia's North Coast / edited by Lou Allison; compiled by Jane Wilde.
Allison, Lou, editor. | Wilde, Jane, 1955- compiler.
Canadiana 20230222668 | ISBN 9781773861180 (softcover)
LCSH: Men—British Columbia—Pacific Coast—Biography. | LCSH: Urban-rural migration—History—20th century. | LCSH: Country life—British Columbia—Pacific Coast. | LCSH: Seafaring life—British Columbia—Pacific Coast. | LCSH: Pacific Coast (B.C.)—Biography. | LCGFT: Biographies.
LCC HQ1090.7.C2 G86 2023 | DDC 305.31092/27111—dc23

Nautical Adventures on British Columbia's North Coast

GUMBOOT GUYS

Edited by Lou Allison
with Jane Wilde

Caitlin Press 2023

Contents

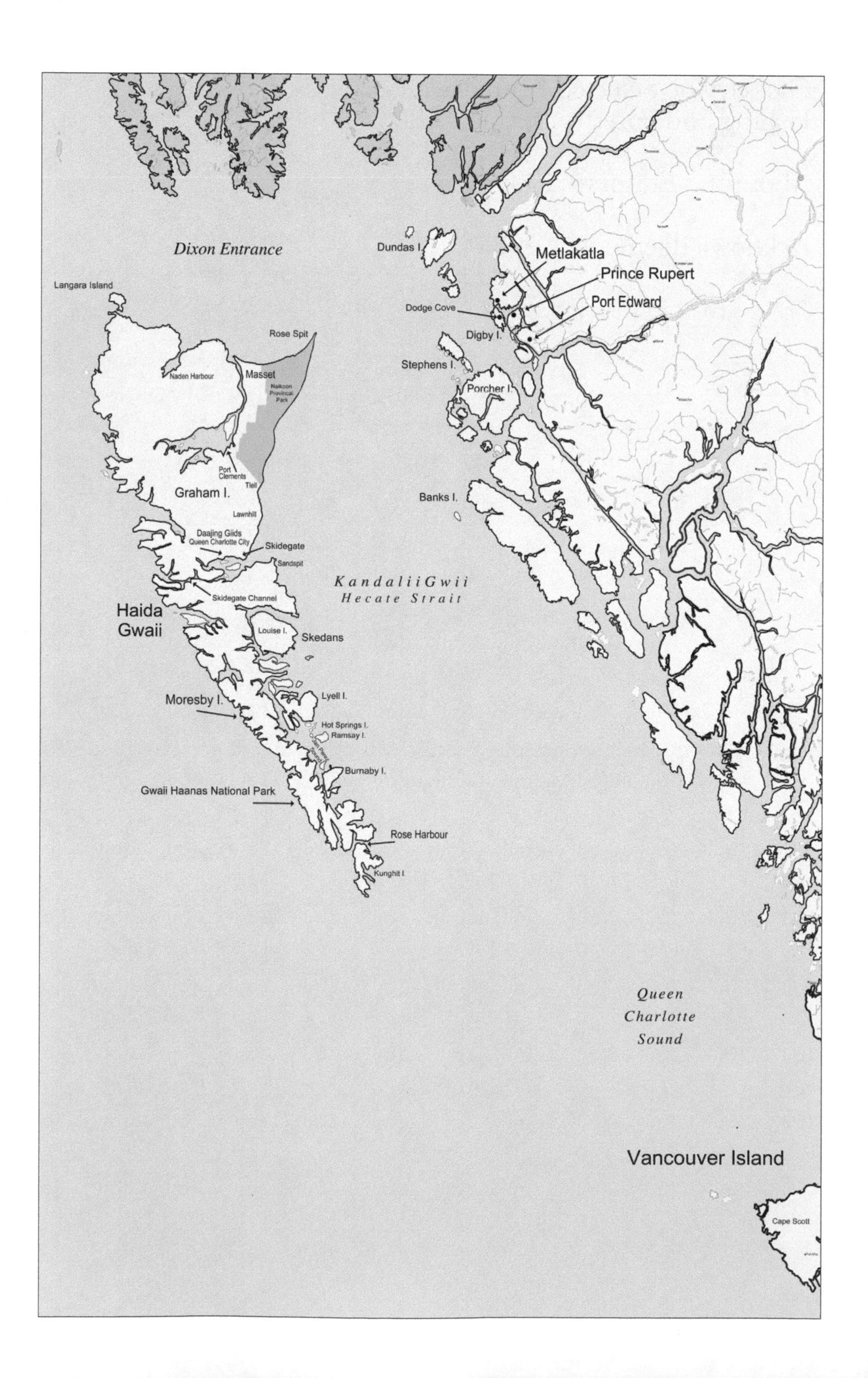

Dixon Entrance
Dundas I.
Metlakatla
Prince Rupert
Port Edward
Dodge Cove
Digby I.
Stephens I.
Porcher I.
Banks I.
Langara Island
Rose Spit
Naden Harbour
Masset
Naikoon Provincial Park
Port Clements
Tlell
Graham I.
Lawnhill
Daajing Giids
Queen Charlotte City
Skidegate
Sandspit
Skidegate Channel
Kandalii Gwii
Hecate Strait
Haida Gwaii
Louise I.
Skedans
Lyell I.
Moresby I.
Hot Springs I.
Ramsay I.
Burnaby I.
Gwaii Haanas National Park
Rose Harbour
Kunghit I.
Queen Charlotte Sound
Vancouver Island
Cape Scott

Land Acknowledgement and a Note Regarding Place Names

The stories in *Gumboot Guys* take place on the land and waters of Haida Gwaii, occupied by the Haida People since time immemorial, on the unceded traditional territory of the Ts'msyen (Tsimshian), including the Lax Kw'alaams Band and the Metlakatla First Nation.

Caitlin Press respectfully acknowledges that it operates on the unceded traditional territory of the Qualicum First Nation and the traditional keepers of their land.

To set these stories in the time in which they took place, we chose to use the names that were in use at that time. However, we feel that it is important to recognize the changes that have taken place. Since the 1970s, many of the place names referred to in these stories have reverted to Indigenous names, and place names used in the seventies are no longer appropriate, except colloquially.

These are the current names of these places along with a very brief description.

Haida Gwaii: Queen Charlotte Islands was officially changed to Haida Gwaii, which means "Islands of the People," in 2010.

Gwaii Haanas: The park that was established in the area of the Haida Gwaii, referred to in the stories variously as "South Moresby" and similar terms, is named the "Gwaii Haanas National Park Reserve, National Marine Conservation Area, and Haida Heritage Site," or simply Gwaii Haanas, which means "Islands of Beauty." The establishment of the Park (or Reserve) had an evolution over more than a decade, and came into being under the current shared management agreement in 1993.

Daajing Giids: Queen Charlotte City was officially changed to Daajing Giids in 2022. The name refers to wearing a hat and means "Cedar Dance Hat" or "The Hat of the Child of a Chief."

Lax Kw'alaams: The name of the Tsimshian community of Port Simpson was officially changed to Lax Kw'alaams, which means "Place of the Wild Roses," in 1986.

For anyone interested in the Indigenous names and their meanings, we encourage further research, particularly on the websites and sources maintained by the Nations.

Jane's Introduction

Jane arriving on Haida Gwaii, wide-eyed, greeted by her elementary school pal Lenny.

In September 2022, I picked up the phone. "Lou, can we do one more book together?"

I knew there were more stories to be told about our 1970s migrations from across North America to the North Coast of BC. In our first book, *Gumboot Girls*, we and other women wrote of our adventures on both sides of Hecate Strait. Some of the men who wrote for this book shared those adventures with us and became lifelong friends, lovers, partners and fathers to our children.

I was curious to know what the men's impressions of those years would be. As the stories flooded in, a recurring theme emerged: boats, always. Living in our North Coast communities, most of us were familiar with, and sometimes completely dependent on, boats for transportation, employment and adventure.

Lou said yes, thirty-two writers said yes and our publisher at Caitlin Press, Vici, said yes, again.

We asked the writers, in sharing their stories and photos, to consider some or all of these questions:

Why did you move to the North Coast in the seventies?

What about your boat?

Who were your influences/social connections/community at the time?

Are any seeds of your original vision evident in your present life?

The writers sent reams of photos and wrote about their experiences of buying, building, working, exploring and forever maintaining, rebuilding and often replacing boats. So much learning, so much work, so much challenge! They also shared stories of the deep connections they made with each other and the communities they moved to. Fifty years later, many are still friends and some are still running boats.

As the stories and photos arrived, they triggered rich memories: each new perspective of our shared coastal experiences of the seventies added to the picture of that heady decade.

Thanks to all of our family and friends who have so helpfully and patiently supported me and Lou through another exciting publishing adventure together!

Lou's Introduction

Lou in the cockpit of a trimaran, sailing in very light winds off Cumshewa Head.

Once again, the indefatigable Jane Wilde, with her abiding interest in the demographic influx of young people to coastal British Columbia in the seventies, felt there were more stories to tease out.

This anthology, our third collection of stories of young people who migrated to the West Coast, takes a new tack. Or should I call it "a different kettle of fish"? The first book, *Gumboot Girls*, concerned young women who arrived on the North Coast, including the Queen Charlotte Islands [Haida Gwaii]. The second, *Dancing in Gumboots*, revolved around central Vancouver Island and a few nearby Gulf Islands. This time, we have returned to the North Coast with the stories of young men who arrived in the area seeking opportunity or adventure, and who became entranced by boats. One such, a friend, described it like this: "For us, it was all boats, all the time." Boats afforded the opportunity to explore beyond the reach of roads, to learn new skills including boatbuilding, navigating, wilderness exploring, commercial fishing and more, and for many, they also meant economic opportunity. The romance of the sea permeated the times: sometimes those dreams came to fruition, sometimes they foundered.

Jane was not sure what we would garner when we sent out the invitation. We have been surprised, amused, appalled and enchanted, turn and turnabout. We hope that you will be as well as you join us on this nautical adventure.

Alp

Jim Horner

As soon as I finished grade twelve in the spring of 1973, I left Toronto. I moved in with a girlfriend in Vancouver and, as a skier, I was anxious to visit Whistler. A friend training for the national ski team had shared stories and pictures of his summer ski camps there. Unfortunately, things did not work out with the girlfriend and I quickly discovered there was no accommodation to be found at Whistler, so I moved on.

As fall approached, after a summer of adventures, I found myself literally at the end of the road. I was down and out, totally humbled, staying at the rowdy Friendship House in Prince Rupert. I was looking into applying for a TV arts course back at Toronto's Ryerson college when my luck changed and a gyppo logger from Port Clements hired and flew me over to the Misty Islands. Within a week, this teenager was making big money operating a log-hauling skidder until Coho Logging shut down for Christmas.

Originally from Toronto, Jim was introduced to commercial fishing by fellow ski bums who worked all summer to finance their winter skiing.

Finally, the snow season arrived and, flush with cash, I headed off island to discover new ski resorts. I ended up skiing in the Swiss Alps in January and February before returning to Canada in March. At both Whistler and Tod Mountain, I rode chairlifts with numerous fishermen ski bums who spoke about working hard commercial fishing all summer to ski every day all winter.

Hmmm… that sounded pretty good!

After walking the fishermen's wharves at Steveston and False Creek, I felt it was obvious that a displaced hippy teenager from Toronto was unlikely to ever get a foot in that door. After a couple of successful years of ski bumming and a very profitable summer job in the Yukon, I returned to the Islands. I caught the ferry in Skagway and returned to Queen Charlotte City [Daajing Giids] in the fall of 1975.

I was able to pay cash for a lot in QCC. I immersed myself in the pleasures of gathering food and enjoying the social scene that this vibrant community offered. There was so much to do and learn in the day, and at night, the potluck dinners, bars and dance halls made for a bustling social scene. It was an easy decision to sacrifice the 1976 ski season to pursue my commercial fishing dreams. I did some carpentry work in Skidegate but mostly worked handlogging out on the west coast with mentor not-so-little "Little Bill" Yahonavich on his boat the *Jessie Falls*.

My next-door neighbour on Hippie Hill, Jane Kinegal, had recently married a fisherman known as KP who owned the salmon troller the *Child of the Moon*. One afternoon, KP pounded on my door, saying that he needed a deckhand and was in a hurry to get out of town. Finally: the break I had been pining for!

Within a few short hours, we were on our way over the Sandspit Bar, heading out to the edge that bisects the centre of Hecate Strait on the east side of Haida Gwaii. Hecate Strait is a nasty place to hang out. Thankfully, after that we mostly fished the traditional grounds off the west coast. I quickly realized that trolling for salmon was no longer just a job to support my ski habit. It was the best job in the world! I was hooked.

After a few more trips to Cape Saint James and the west side, we took a few days off. We needed to put the boat up on the tidal grid to do some bottom work. As I was walking down from Hippie Hill the next morning, with gear bag in hand, expecting to go back to sea, I saw the *Child of the Moon* smoking full speed across Bearskin Bay. It was west coast–bound without me, star deckhand and bringer of good luck. FUCK! I was so pissed in the moment, but as always, all bad things lead to good. Oh well, at least now I had some experience as a deckhand on a commercial

Jim restored the derelict fishing troller *Alp* to its former glory. The night before they were due to leave the dock, shore workers voted to strike.

salmon troller. Unfortunately, I was one short of being eligible for collecting unemployment insurance (UIC, as it was then called). Had I been eligible, I would have probably gone back to Whistler. Instead, thankfully, I remained another full year.

I kept busy feathering my new nest with homemade chainsaw lumber and handlogging or banging nails to get by. I was hoping to find another job on a salmon troller but by spring nothing had materialized.

At that time, a retired fisherman/boatbuilder named Ed Regnery, whom everyone called Rags, lived with his wife just up from the docks. Rags was working on a new boat and had got the government to sponsor a woman who was taking a boatbuilding course off island to come and help. Her name was Sue Wells and, as we enjoyed each other's company, I tended to hang at Rags's shed. One day, Rags told me about a derelict boat called the *Alp*, a double-ended salmon troller that had been pulled up on the beach across from the high school. He mentioned that the chances of me getting another deckhand job on a troller were slim and that the *Alp* could probably be bought for the price of the government fishing licence. He went on and on about how it was a famously good sea boat, had a nearly new diesel engine and, most importantly, was very fishy. "Fishy" means being a good producer: in trolling, some boats repel salmon, some attract. My interest was now seriously piqued; I drove down to survey the old boat.

Although its cosmetics were a mess, like a face that only a mother could love, I was immediately smitten with its potential. The *Alp* had been my friends the Kuleshas' first troller and they were now among the top highliners of the local fleet. They had installed a new diesel engine and told me that the boat "just caught too many fish for its size." While crawling around inside, I was puzzled by some of the gizmos, levers, valves, gauges and meters. Being able to look right through the deck where it had been bashed apart on both sides didn't intimidate me. If anything, as a wood butcher, I was just as stoked about learning how to refit the boat as I was about going fishing with it. The prospect of an opportunity to work with wood in a whole new way really turned my crank. Rags built up my confidence by offering his services. He suggested that I hire him to come by to oversee the project for an hour or so a day. I am so grateful to have been a pawn in his self-employment strategy!

Bill Valentine, the principal of the high school, owned the boat. When the school bell rang, I went over to meet him and make him my offer, the value of the fishing licence. He accepted without a moment's thought and almost shook my arm off. He also offered me the use of the school's well-tooled wood and metal shop after school hours.

Unfortunately, I was pretty naive at the time about banks and how to secure a loan. I wasted precious days that turned into weeks waiting for my local credit union's board to make its negative decision almost a month later. Although at the time the loan was guaranteed by the government, I guess now that they knew how little experience the long-haired kid from Toronto had. After the rejection, I remember sitting, dejected, in Margaret's Café. I shared a table with a mild-mannered gentleman by the name of Andy Whitmore, Charlotte's notary public. When I told him my tale of woe, he trash talked me.

"You really want that rotten derelict? Then get off your ass and get a haircut and a shirt that has a collar, fly over to Prince Rupert, visit the banks, tell the bankers what you need and tell them you need it now! And be sure to let them know that the credit union strung you along wasting a month of your precious time."

I flew over to Rupert the next day and crashed at Orlan Ralph's new place that had previously been a morgue. I slept in a room that used to store dead people. I got a haircut and a collared shirt from the Sally Ann. With Andy's confidence, Rags's handwritten survey of the boat, the licence papers, the blue book and the deed to my land, in case I needed it, I went banking. By noon, with nothing down, I had secured my loan, my estimate of enough money to rebuild the *Alp* and purchase a new radar.

By that point, pretty much a month had passed since I first fell in love with the *Alp*. The long delay cost me dearly as there was so much work to get it seaworthy, let alone fishing. A few boats were already heading out to the grounds. To start off, Rags and I drove my green work truck, dubbed Celery, up coast and ordered a load of specialty lumber from Bill McKay's mill by Tlell. Rags wanted fire-killed, seasoned, quarter-sawn, edge-grain, clear western red cedar for planking material that matched the thickness of the *Alp*'s old planking. Also an order of clear yellow cedar for ribs, beams and bulkheads. I had to order Honduras gumwood for rail caps and a new shoe the length of the keel to be shipped up on the *Northland Prince* from Vancouver. Gumwood planks weigh almost as much and are almost as tough as steel. Bill Valentine graciously provided a new stainless drive shaft that he had ordered earlier. While waiting for all that to arrive, I built a plastic roof over the whole boat and, on both sides, scaffolding that even Rags (with his Dutch-wooden-shoed, bedroom-slippered, swollen and arthritic feet) could navigate.

Once the materials arrived, I finally started rebuilding, but only after the painful job of removing rotten wood. It was like opening a can of worms as I had to keep removing more and more until I finally got down to sound wood. The scope of the project had grown and I could see how immense my job really was. I ordered more lumber and strung up more light bulbs.

I would get in a decently productive morning shift before picking up Rags at ten. He would usually be there for an hour each day unless we were steaming planks and he would stay until after lunch. His routine was to first inspect what I had accomplished and then go on about how in his day he could do at least twice as much. Then he would give me the advice and direction I so desperately needed. He would always discreetly give me a little pep talk each time I would drive him home. He helped keep my head on straight and focussed each step of the way.

Finally, the *Alp*'s hull was all closed in and watertight, so it was time to hire the Dingwall brothers, Bill and Ben, with their D8 Cat to push it out on its log-grid cradle onto the beach at low tide. The rising tide would set it afloat. We christened it well and the re-corked seams hardly leaked a drop.

The next day, May 14, was my birthday. Marg put together a full-house, surprise birthday dinner party for me at the café, a smorgasbord of seafood and venison. After dinner, we all walked down to the Charlotte Recreation Centre to see Sonny Terry and Brownie McGee play live. Good times!

In the following days, a parade of fishermen would stop by at the dock to inspect the *Alp* and offer advice. Rags didn't like the look of the bottom of the mast, so I cut it back inch by inch until the rot was gone. We then fashioned a very tall mast base from a well-seasoned piece of yellow cedar.

At long last, the *Alp* was all fuelled, iced and grubbed up; miraculously, we were finally ready to go. One last night in town with my new-found girlfriend/deckhand and we could finally cast off in the morning.

After dinner, I heard a lot of commotion coming down the ramp. It was a group of wives of gillnet fishermen shouting that the union had voted to strike: "Tie her up! Tie her up!"

I naively thought to myself, *Right, sure thing. After all this, I'm going to cancel my plans to catch the tide out to the west side in the morning because a bunch of shore workers or net fishers are not happy. What the fuck?*

I went up to the bar, fishers all greeting me with, "Too bad about the strike, hope it's not a long one." I spoke with a troller who said he had sat out lots of strikes even though most of the troll fleet are not union members. He said, "The shore workers we sell to are unionized and if you

Jim owned and fished the *Alp* for twelve years, and much of that time was spent in the misty waters of Haida Gwaii.

go out, they will put you on the scab list and then you can't sell to them anymore." Rags once again calmed me down.

The strike only lasted three or four days and I really did still have lots to keep me busy on the boat. The whole fleet had to come into town to tie up, so I had a lot of experienced talent helping me fine tune my new lean, mean, fishing machine.

My first trip out to the west coast was unforgettable. I was lucky I had the new radar and a gal on the wheel as it was so foggy it felt like we were inside a ping-pong ball. My lures were all old and tarnished and I even had some of the hooks on backwards. Nevertheless, they worked and caught as many large red spring salmon as I could possibly keep up with. We ended up bringing in a decent load.

My new deckhand/girlfriend didn't care to go back out to the cold, foggy west side and carried on with her summer travels across Canada. Now that the *Alp* and I had proven ourselves, I was able to hire Herb Hughan, who had once owned his own troller. Herb came out with me for two trips before he had to head up to the Nass. He, too, taught me a lot.

I owned and fished the *Alp* for the next twelve years, eight of which I was accompanied by Anne-Marie and then Fran. Some of my fondest memories were fishing with these two amazing women. Anything I could do, they could do better. Sadly, in 1988 the *Alp* sank in the deepest hole of the Salish Sea with a deck load of spring salmon. I owned two more salmon trollers over the next twelve years. For a quarter of a century, I never worked a single winter.

These were the glory years of working hard, fishing the west side of Haida Gwaii for four months a summer and filling my passport and skiing the other eight.

Hmmm… that was pretty good!

Excerpted from Jim's unpublished memoir Eighteen Lives.

Argo

Greg Martin

How I learned to hate sailing: it started in 1971 with an eight-foot wooden boat. My partner, Bayla, had fond memories of sailing on a thirty-eight-foot ketch in San Francisco Bay during her residency in family medicine. She thought that we should buy a little sailboat, a Sabot, that she found in Port Clements. We tied it to the roof of her VW Beetle to get it home to Queen Charlotte City [Daajing Giids].

The layout of the little boat included a bench affixed from side to side (athwart ship, I later learned), which secured both the mast and keel board, as well as prevented anyone from going forward. So, Bayla and I sat in the rear of the boat, which caused the Sabot to be very low in the stern. I later learned that this class of sailing dinghy was designed to be raced competitively by an anemic twelve-year-old in either a very calm lake or in a very large bathtub, certainly not by two naive adults in the Pacific Ocean.

We lived in a small log cabin on the beach in the west end of QCC, surrounded by the MacMillan Bloedel log boom, with no electricity, six-mil plastic for window glazing and an outhouse for plumbing. It was very romantic.

Greg poses next to the little Sabot sailing dinghy, bought in Port Clements and delivered to Daajing Giids on the roof of Bayla's VW Beetle.

One day, we launched the boat from our beach and sailed out into the bay. There was a nice breeze and we were thrilled as the wind filled our sail. The boat heeled over from the breeze and a wave came over the side and swamped the boat, which then capsized. We were both wearing life jackets and tried to climb onto the upside-down hull but there wasn't enough buoyancy to support either one of us. The water was very cold, so we started swimming toward the log boom. Because we were wet and numb, we couldn't pull ourselves up onto the slippery logs, so we stayed in the water and pulled ourselves along until we made it to our beach and then to our cabin and some dry clothes. After the boat washed ashore, we sold it.

Using my male intuition, the obvious answer to this situation was to buy a bigger, safer boat. The following year, armed with a five-thousand-dollar loan approval from our local Canadian Imperial Bank of Commerce (CIBC) branch, I travelled to Vancouver and bought the *Argo*, a twenty-five-foot wooden sloop. In the early seventies, I wore gumboots daily, even when on the mainland. When I was in the Vancouver CIBC branch to claim the money transfer to purchase the vessel, the teller phoned our QCC CIBC branch to confirm my identity. The QCC teller advised her Vancouver counterpart to see if I was wearing black gumboots. The teller came out from behind the counter and looked at my feet. I have always found Vancouver a bit strange. My identity was confirmed and I received the certified cheque for the purchase.

The *Argo* was twenty years old and equipped with a 1952 Atomic 4 inboard auxiliary, which was a rather primitive, flathead gas-powered engine. I never did figure out the "Atomic" part. The navigation system consisted of a compass and a portable, battery-powered multiband radio with radio direction finding (RDF) capability. There was no depth sounder, but after I brought the *Argo* home, my friend Karl Kulesha gave me a very old and heavy Ekolite flasher-type depth sounder, a hand-me-down from his commercial fishing vessel, the *Alp*. The Ekolite had a hypnotic, rotating strobe light for a display and was the pride of the Allied navies for submarine detection in World War II. It could sometimes indicate the depth but rarely showed fish. I always felt confident that it could detect a large, submerged, steel-hulled submarine beneath me.

When it was time for me to take possession of the *Argo* and bring it home to Haida Gwaii (!), my dear friend Illtyd Perkins volunteered to help me. Illtyd was a retired literature professor, accomplished boatbuilder, sailor and all-round polymath. The *Argo* was moored at Secret Cove. When Illtyd and I set about getting it ready for the trip home, his first inspection highlighted the widespread rot in the cabin roof and decks. *Gulp!*

We set sail for home. Well, truthfully, we didn't sail the whole time: we used our "Atomic-powered" auxiliary a lot. While Illtyd was a very skilled sailor, I discovered that I felt extremely uncomfortable when the *Argo* was heeled over under sail. I was having flashbacks to the Sabot sinking beneath me. I was having post-traumatic sailing disorder, also known as PTSD.

We had a very calm, windless day for crossing the Hecate Strait and motored over to the Charlottes, homing in on the Lawn Point radio beacon with our RDF. We tied the *Argo* up at the QCC dock and headed home for showers and clean clothes. The next day, the Atomic 4 would not start but the starter motor turned the engine over at great speed. A compression test revealed that there was NO compression. We had used up the engine's last bit of life crossing the Hecate. I ordered parts to rebuild the Atomic 4 on the cheap.

Once the *Argo* had power again, Illtyd guided me through the process of removing the rotten parts of the decks and cabin. A local fisherman very kindly loaned us his intertidal boat cradle and we put the *Argo* up on a high tide. We removed the mast, rigging and the decks and cabin. The *Argo* now looked like an open, twenty-five-foot canoe!

On a calm, windless day, Greg motored his new wooden sloop, the *Argo*, across the Hecate Strait to its new port at Haida Gwaii.

Because we had no electricity at home, my workshop was one-third of the ground floor of the building housing Bayla's medical office. This building, locally known as the Rainbows building, is located on Oceanview Drive at Alder Street. It had previously been a Chinese restaurant and my workshop was located where the kitchen had been. I wasn't allowed to run power tools during office hours as Bayla thought it might upset her patients. I had to work mostly in the evenings, laminating cabin beams and pre-forming wooden components.

Over the next few years, I spent much more time restoring the *Argo* than cruising, and even less time sailing. I was able

After discovering that he wasn't that fond of sailing, Greg sold the *Argo* and purchased an aluminum skiff.

to sell the boat to a nice young couple who, unlike me, actually liked sailing. I was ready for a change, from wood to welded aluminum. Although it took our ancestors more than a thousand years to progress from the Bronze Age to the Iron Age, I was able to transition to my own Aluminum Age in just a few short years.

My first aluminum boat was a twenty-four-foot herring skiff, from which I gillnetted herring for a few seasons. It looked like the sort of ice-cube tray that a giant would like and we used it for summer camping trips, salmon trolling and even transporting a 1956 Chevy panel truck to power a sawmill on Kumdis Island.

My current aluminum boat, the motor vessel *Low Island*, is a bit smaller and mostly used for fishing on the west coast of Haida Gwaii. It was built locally by Keith Rowsell and is both fast and stable. And it doesn't heel over in the wind!

Azurite

Jeremiah Randall

1959, Middleborough, Massachusetts, USA, eight years old: I really wanted a small boat to explore the shores of a reservoir inhabited by bullfrogs and turtles, but that didn't happen.

A few years later: my grandparents lived on Tispaquin Pond and my aunt had an eight-foot aluminum skiff with a six-horsepower Evinrude outboard that she let me and my younger cousin use as much as we wanted. One of us ran the boat as fast as possible while the other stood on shore and hit a tennis ball with a wooden golf club as hard as he could. The kid in the boat would zoom to the ball, scoop it out of the water, zoom back at top speed and throw it at the one standing on shore. We traded turns. Eventually, I went west to BC; my cousin stayed in the east. We both became loggers and we're still close. He is like a brother to me.

I moved around BC a fair bit and eventually found the coast, where winters aren't as cold and there are boats. I got a falling job in a camp on Nootka Island just north of Friendly Cove. Fallers work six-and-a-half-hour days and start very early during fire season, so I had time after work to use a boat much like the one on Tispaquin Pond. Instead of zooming after tennis balls, I explored caves.

The summer of 1972, I got a job working for Lindy Jacobsen on a troller called the *Eventide #1*. After I helped him re-install a Scania-Vabis in-line-six engine and paint the boat inside and out, we went to Vancouver then off the west coast of Vancouver Island in the Ucluelet area. Between the oil fumes venting into the engine room and the motion of the swells, I had to be brought back to shore, too sick to work. So, from 1972 to 1978, not much boat travel, except for one trip in 1975, when I delivered a boat

The skiff provided a place to relax during an evening of cruising after a long day of falling trees.

from Vancouver to Comox with the help of a stranger I met on the dock who couldn't steer straight.

A longer-than-usual falling job in Leo Creek, just north of Fort Saint James, earned me enough money to buy either a boat or a horse. I knew I didn't want to live in a town. I wanted to be where I thought I would find the most freedom, either land or sea. I decided out on the ocean and, as I get seasick, I needed a boat of my own, so I was off to Prince Rupert to look for a boat. The year 1978 was a heady time. The town was booming with people from everywhere working in the canneries.

When I met Orlan Ralph, who was renting the bottom floor of a big, old house in Grenville Court and who also had ties to the Haida Gwaii community, he introduced me to Fred. Fred taught me a lot about what to look for and what being a mariner really meant. He introduced me to the book *A Guide for Coastal Navigation*, which became my textbook, and with the help of friends, I eventually found the *Azurite*, a sixty-foot retired packer built in 1913, just after my grandparents were born. The boat had worked hard for decades and was well respected. By now, I was hearing a lot of others' opinions and questions. Fred told me that the boat had a lot of rot but had been well built and that if I didn't pound it into weather it should last. The British-made Gardner 6L3 engine was a draw: those who knew the make were impressed.

Buzzy Stewart, the owner, wanted $6,000 but would take $4,000, and he and his brother would keep the new anchor, anchor rode and a piece of one-inch Samson braid line, not good. While thinking about this as I walked downtown to go have lunch at the West End, I met Linda, a friend from Haida Gwaii who introduced me to Del Fowler. They were over to look at a boat in Port Edward. In conversation, it came out that I needed another $2,000 to purchase the *Azurite* and, right there on the sidewalk, Del asked me if I wanted to partner with him on a handlogging claim. That would be the best job for the right kind of faller, so the deal was struck on a handshake. Out came a roll of cash and I had the $2,000 I needed.

So: buy the *Azurite*. Figure out the Gardner engine. Check out the running gear. Move aboard. Find out that the steering tiller arm is just barely being held by a big nut: the threads on the rudder post are so big and coarse I can clean them with a small cold chisel, tapping round and round. Charge the batteries, four eight-volts linked to make thirty-two. The Gardner starts up easily but overheats almost immediately and I don't know why.

There are a lot of good and smart old guys around the dock who help me, passing me from one to the other for advice. The boss of the machine shop at the Oceanside Cannery gives me all the Gardner books that were on the shelf, as there were no longer any of those engines in the fleet. A mechanic comes over to see if he can help and, with the help of the manuals, finds that the freshwater pump is put together wrong. With that fixed and some adjusting of valves, the engine now runs at temperature. So, even though there is still some sticking in the steering chain, we decide to go for a boat ride.

We untie from the dock and, wow, this is a big boat! We head out of the harbour, not too far. Just opposite Spire Ledge, we decide to turn around and find that the sticking in the steering chain isn't getting better. We feel that we had better get back to the dock and investigate; then, just inside the breakwater at the Fairview dock, the steering chain breaks. We sure couldn't paddle back to the dock! The *Sunfjord*, a big, strong boat with a Viking captain and crew, comes alongside. The captain, looking down on us from the top deck, can read our inexperience and offers to put us back onto the dock in the boat's spot in front of the shipyard. It is done very smoothly.

I found out that the steering chain broke where it went through the steel reinforcement on the bulkhead between the engine room and the fish hold. It was worn and rusted on both the port and starboard sides, so out it came, about thirty-seven metres of a 3/8-inch chain laid out on the dock. It wasn't hard to repair with new pieces of chain put in with repair links.

What I didn't know was how the local people were watching all this. I found out years later that one old guy had remarked, "That guy should be knocked in the head before he kills someone." Word got out that I planned to "cross the Hecate Strait in that rotten old thing."

Fred was getting close to returning to Haida Gwaii in a powerful tug named the *Renner Pass* and told me to be ready because the *Azurite* was going too, either under power or at the end of a tow line. He advised

The *Azurite*, built in 1913, had worked hard for decades. The wooden helm was a classic.

Jeremiah, his girlfriend and their son lived aboard the *Azurite*: the small boy standing on the deck, with his hands on his head, is barely visible in this photo of the vessel docked in Cow Bay.

that it would be better if I learned and figured out the course and ran it myself. Then I could get back or go anywhere else for that matter.

And we did cross, myself and two friends. The first day, we made Larsen Harbour at the north end of Banks Island. We waited a day for perfect weather, then left. Fred and family let us go first.

So started my life on the water. The first job was handlogging with Del and Linda on a claim in Long Arm Inlet. I would fall and limb ten or twenty trees, Linda would yard them in with the *Belle Adventure* and Del ran the skiff. We boomed them after lunch.

When the *Azurite* came to the end of its days, my spouse and I helped Jim McAlister, an amazing welder/fabricator and really good man, build a fifty-seven-foot steel pinky schooner in Oona River on Porcher Island, before hydro came to the community. The *Reach* took us up and down the coast for decades. After that first handlogging job, many more followed: working for logging companies large and small, handlogging with others and by myself, operating tugs and crew boats, falling timber for towers, helicopters and one of the last working A-frames on the coast, beachcombing for logs, hauling fuel and supplies, towing, packing, sampling and monitoring for the Pacific geoduck and urchin fisheries, and monitoring for the spot prawn fishery, often with my spouse, sometimes alone, occasionally with others.

The ocean has been a constant in my life since 1978 to the present day.

Bertha

Orlan Ralph

I spent my childhood years growing up in North Burnaby, very close to Burnaby Lake and Deer Lake. This was before the 401 Freeway was built. To go into the city, we could catch the tram into Vancouver or New Westminster from our Sprott Street station at a cost of four cents, child's fare. We were always building rafts and playing on one of the lakes.

Later, I took a five-year apprenticeship with Austin Metal Fabricators as a sheet metal worker. They asked me if I would like to go to Terrace and do the HVAC (Heating, Ventilation and Air Conditioning) on a couple of jobs. I jumped at the chance as I was in my mid-twenties and ready for some adventure in my life. When I got to the job site, I met a young carpenter named Jerome Auriat, a local. We are still good friends today. There was a long weekend coming up, so Jerome said that we should fly

Mast-raising day requires all hands on deck. With his experience in construction and metal work, Orlan was ready to build his own boat.

over to Haida Gwaii for the three days. We flew from Prince Rupert to Masset. When we got to the dock in Masset, we were told that we could stay at a house owned by Sydney Smith at the top of the dock. There, we met David Phillips, who was looking after the B&B for Sydney. David spent the night telling us all about the Islands.

The next day, we decided to hitchhike down to Daajing Giids (then called Queen Charlotte City). It was very easy in those days to hitch a ride. The person who picked us up also stopped in Tlell and picked up an older guy with a grey blanket wrapped around him. His name was Hibby Gren, a local poet. Hibby got us to stop at Saint Mary's Spring. He told us to have a drink from the spring, as it was a legend that if we drank from the spring we would return to the Islands. He was right about that. We got dropped off at Margaret's Café. This was the local spot to find out about anything you wanted in town. I could easily see that there was a lot of good energy here and that I was coming back for sure.

I finished the two jobs that I had in Terrace, went back to Burnaby and decided to move to Haida Gwaii. How could I not with the introduction I had to the Islands? I found a cabin to rent in Daajing Giids from Rudy Gasdigger. I had always wanted to build a boat and this seemed to be a good place to do it. Rudy was good enough to let me build a boatshed on his property. In those days, it was easy to go out to the logged areas and gather small cut cedars for poles and larger blocks of cedar to hand-split shakes. As I started to build the shed, I met Ron Wall, who also wanted to build a boat, a twenty-seven-foot sailing dory that he already had the plans for. Ron helped finish the boatshed and we built the two boats side by side. The hulls and the sails were the same design but the cabins were different. We finished and launched our boats around the same time too. I named my boat the *Bertha*; it just seemed to fit.

Margaret's Café was the spot for chocolate cake soaked in condensed milk, with a side of local gossip.

To support myself while building my boat, I would go to Prince Rupert or Terrace to work in construction. In Rupert, I rented the downstairs of 37

Orlan built the twenty-seven-foot dory, named *Bertha*, using plans designed by John Gardner.

Grenville Court located pretty much in the centre of downtown. There, I met many of the boat people who lived in Dodge Cove, Crippen Cove and Salt Lakes, as a lot of the Rupert clan were renting the upstairs. I am sure a lot of you who were around in those days will remember this place, as there was never a dull moment. A lot of the Haida Gwaii clan would stay with me when they came over.

I spent a total of fourteen great years on Haida Gwaii.

Callistratus

Hans Elfert

Like many other North Coast boys, I spent a few years of my youth deck-handing on fishboats, tugboats and other vessels like the Canadian Coast Guard buoy tender the *Alexander Mackenzie*. Eventually, I ended up fabricating and welding equipment for the new and explosively growing herring roe fishing industry.

The herring roe business brought many Japanese businessmen to BC. It was during a conversation between one of these businessmen, who was perhaps a bit bolder than others in offering his opinion, and Sid Dickens and Dave Lorette, two fishermen of the Prince Rupert Fishermen's Co-operative, that he derided the state of our fishing industry and its vessels. He issued a challenge: "Why don't you come to Japan and see how it should be done?" Sid and Dave accepted and went to Japan at the invitation of one of the Japanese herring roe companies to see the Japanese fishing boats and industry.

In 1976, the Canadian minister of state announced a two-hundred-mile fishing limit. Many countries were enacting similar legislation. In

Before gaining enough experience in welding and fabrication to work on large vessels, Hans spent a few years as a deckhand.

Canada, it took effect on January 1, 1977, and, as a result, dozens of huge factory trawlers that had been operating in our waters were expelled. This seemed to suggest that there should be room for one small factory trawler to operate in BC waters. Although there were Canadian trawlers working on our coast, they were mostly smaller boats delivering poor-quality fish, with the exception of a few boats using ice. The existing trawlers tended to be boats delivering fish that had been sloshing around in large tanks full of water for a week before being brought to shore plants for processing.

Soon, the local entrepreneurs were looking to buy a second-hand Japanese factory trawler. However, it seemed that Japanese fishing vessels were built for an average life of eight years, so any vessel they could find was already a rather rusty hulk with too many missing bits for Canadian waters and bureaucrats. Gradually, the project became one of building a new trawler using whatever second-hand equipment could be found in the huge fleet of fishing vessels around Japan. This required more partners and a whole lot more money.

Knowing my experience in building equipment for the fishing industry and my experience on a few fishboats, Sid and Dave approached me to join them as a partner in this ambitious project. It had been decided that each partner would have to raise $250,000 and since I had practically none of that my family helped me borrow the money. Another fisherman, Buck Hemmons, joined the project and, in the summer of 1978, we were off to Japan to start the adventure. A few days of intense discussions and negotiations, lubricated by a lot of socializing in clubs and restaurants of Tokyo, led to the signing of contracts for the building of a new trawler. Next came a week around a big table in Tokyo with at least a dozen engineers, architects and technicians to work out the design of the new vessel, based on the standard 454-tonne class trawler of which hundreds had been built in Japan over the preceding decades. In our case, however, the vessel became 635 registered tonnes and 193 feet long.

Next came a short whirlwind trip to Europe to look at refrigeration, fish processing, decks and other machinery for the boat. It was my first return to Europe since I left Germany as a three-year-old.

Once the construction began, I returned to Japan, to Muroran on the north island of Hokkaidō where the shipyard Narasaki Senpakukogyo was located. The seven months I spent there supervising the construction of the vessel was one of the most mind-opening and exciting times of my life. I was given a small apartment near the shipyard and walked there every morning and back again at night. For the first few weeks, I was constantly taken out to restaurants and clubs after work as the Japanese are famous for their hospitality. Gradually that waned and I became more independent and able to shop and look after myself. Everywhere I went I found people excited and enthusiastic about my growing knowledge of Japanese and eager to help me learn more. On my way home from the shipyard in the afternoon, if I stopped at the fence around the schoolyard I went by, a crowd of children would quickly surround me. They would giggle and ask questions like, "Are you a rock star?"

Friday evenings I would head out to a nearby *unagi* shop, one of 10,000 across Japan, for a bowl of *unadon*. This was a simple bowl of rice with a few pieces of barbecued eel on top and some special sauce. It had become my favourite among the enormous number of different foods the Japanese offered me. I ate and enjoyed almost everything to the great delight of my hosts, who were accustomed to *gaijin* (foreigners) having great difficulty with raw fish and many other delicacies that were, at that time, still quite unknown in the West.

The work in the shipyard proceeded quite rapidly and I had to be alert and scramble around everywhere to catch things that might need changing. One morning, for example, I went down into the engine room to discover a small water pipe going right across a passage on the port side of the engine. It was at my eye level but well over the head of the pipefitter who installed it. Of course, he had to reroute it.

The biggest part of my effort in the yard, however, went into the preparation and painting of the ship. The Japanese paid very little attention to the painting of their fishing vessels because they would work them continuously for seven or eight years, then melt them down and make new ones. That is why all the older vessels we saw in Japan were rusting hulks.

To keep costs down, however, we did find some used equipment, such as the Akasaka main engine, a great engine that served us very well throughout the time we had it. In fact, that engine remained in the *Callistratus* until the end of her life in 2017. Some of the winches and other deck machinery were also purchased second-hand. We travelled to Niigata, Sendai and Yaizu to look for parts. The Shinkansen train that took us there, at three hundred kilometres per hour, was still fairly new and the marvel of the age.

The keel laying and launching of the *Callistratus* was accompanied by elaborate but perfunctory Shinto ceremonies. It was amusing to see the Shinto priests taking their smoke break from work like any other shipyard worker.

Several weeks before the vessel was finished, we asked the shipyard to find some old, heavy and discarded chain that we could use to make weight clumps for our nets. As the launch date approached, we asked a few more times but nothing came. Suddenly, two days before our departure, a truck arrived with a couple tonnes of bright, shiny, brand new galvanized chain. We were a little surprised but assumed that they had, at the last minute, simply grabbed some chain from stores. The chain was stowed away on board without further thought. We left Japan on New Year's Day, 1979.

When the *Callistratus* arrived in Prince Rupert, it was greeted by a flotilla of boats of all sorts and sizes. Among that flotilla were some small boats from Salt Lakes, Dodge Cove and Crippen Cove, just across the harbour. In one of these small skiffs was Margo Watkins, a fisheries biologist who lived in Salt Lakes. She had already been going out on trawlers as a biologist/researcher for some time and her boss, Nev Venables, assigned her to that job on the *Callistratus*. The Department of Fisheries and Oceans Canada (DFO) asked Margo to deliver the licence for the *Callistratus* but Nev declined, as her role was only for research and it was only at the discretion of the vessel that she was able to go out on it. Nev likely refused their request

The laying and launching of the *Callistratus* was marked by elaborate Shinto ceremonies. The crew left Japan on New Year's Day, 1979.

because he knew or suspected there was an issue with the licence and he didn't want Margo to be the bearer of bad news. As a result, the DFO flew a functionary to Prince Rupert to present the papers.

Once we finally got out fishing, we looked at our licence for the first time and discovered that it prohibited us from fishing inside the twelve-mile limit, which effectively prevented us from catching bottom fish in BC. That had not been part of our agreement with the DFO when we went to build the boat in Japan.

When we started fishing, we towed our net across what we thought was safe bottom. Suddenly, the boat lurched ahead and the warps went slack. We pulled the warps aboard with only a few remnants of net attached. We had lost our whole net without having noticed any hang-up on the bottom. In our wheelhouse was a brand new, recently invented gadget, a Loran-C plotter pen that recorded our passage over the bottom on a thirty-centimetre square piece of paper. I quickly welded up a grapple out of some shafting and six pieces of 3/4 inch round bar. We attached it to our warp, lowered it to the bottom and began to carefully retrace our path along the pen marks on our plotter.

Margo, who was aboard as an observer, had recently been on a trawler that had lost its gear and had stayed with them for a week as they tried to retrieve it with a large grapple and no success. She looked at our puny grapple and went to bed. A few hours later, she was awakened by someone knocking at her door.

"Suzy, Suzy,"—she had acquired the nickname Suzy Seagull because some captains couldn't remember her name—"we got the net back and there are fish in it!"

A new way of trawling: hang up your net on the bottom and wait for the fish. We had used pieces of that shiny new chain from Japan to assemble the net and connect it to the doors. The chain was actually defective and had failed testing after galvanizing. It was still good for weight clumps, but not under load.

We flailed around for a few months trying to find and catch some fish outside the twelve-mile limit with very poor results. Finally, we decided that the only fish we were allowed to catch in sufficient quantity were the hake that only a few boats were interested in. That, however, required a major rebuilding of our processing space to accommodate both headed and gutted fish, and even a full-fledged filleting, skinning and block pan freezing operation. That required quite a bit of time and a lot more money to install and eventually involved the arrival of some new partners, all members of the Prince Rupert Fishermen's Co-operative.

The Daily News

PUBLISHED AT CANADA'S MOST STRATEGIC PACIFIC PORT
"PRINCE RUPERT, THE KEY TO THE GREAT NORTHWEST"

69TH YEAR NO. 10 PRINCE RUPERT, B.C., MONDAY, JANUARY 15, 1979 624-6781 Price 25 Cents

B.C. and Alaska Conference

Fishermen agree to discuss problems

A three-day Prince Rupert conference, deemed both historic and significant by the representatives of various fishing industry unions and federations from B.C. and Alaska attending the meeting, ended mid-day Sunday with a resolve to maintain lines of communication on common problems.

At the close of the meeting, George Hewison, secretary-treasurer of the United Fishermen's and Allied Workers' Union (UFAWU) said he appreciated the fact that the meeting had led to such a good exchange and added that he found the forum more useful than having to communicate through bureaucracies.

Comparison of fishermen's licencing and salmon enhancement schemes were topics which generated much of the discussion during the three days, although fish prices, organization structure, bilateral fisheries negotiations and oil spills were also addressed.

In a statement released at the end of the conference, delegates jointly expressed a shared concern over the growing concentration of capital and its affects on fishermen and fish processing, and also said they would work more closely in future to oppose any oil pipeline schemes which would increase the risk of spills with the resultant damage to the fishery resource of both countries.

Canadian and U.S. fishermen, but the capital expenditure required to catch and process the bottom-fish species previously taken by foreign vessels, was considered a major problem.

On Saturday, talks turned to a comparison of licencing procedures, and an expression of common concern over foreign intervention and pollution.

In the U.S., licences are awarded to a fisherman rather than a particular boat, a system perceived as more reasonable and flexible by delegates from both nations.

In regards to foreign investment, the Japanese presence was the main topic of discussion.

"Here, it is a matter of the Japanese bankrolling industry, whereas in Alaska it is a matter of the Japanese actually coming in and taking over physical control of certain companies," UFAWU president Jack Nichols said in an interview Saturday.

"We both see some dangers in this. While there is no question of the short term benefits, we question what the long-term effect is going to be."

POLLUTION CONSIDERED

Pollution was considered mainly in the form of oil spills from tanker traffic carrying Alaska crude to refineries in Washington State.

"If there was an oil spill off the Queen Charlotte Islands in Dixon Entrance, it could well

Rupert, had been organized by Hewison.

Nichols said he would meet with the UFAWU board this week and would recommend that the union disassociate itself from the negotiations.

"We're not prepared to sit still for this sort of thing," he said.

Nichols said that the Native Brotherhood of B.C., the other major representative of fishermen in the negotiations, had indicated its support for the UFAWU position and has said it, too, would consider withdrawing from the talks.

ALASKA PANHANDLE

Nichols told the Alaskan delegates that the government's public and private positions concerning negotiations in regard to the stock from Alaska Panhandle streams seemed at variance.

He said negotiators at the U.S.-Canada talks were willing to forget entirely stocks from the Panhandle streams, while Skeena MP Iona Campagnolo has denied that the government has given up the value of Panhandle fish.

In response, Alaskan delegates said they were concerned that the U.S. negotiators were more worried about Washington State fishermen than Alaskan fishermen. Larry Cotter said there was a general desire to negotiate an Alaskan-Canadian treaty separate from the Canada-U.S. negotiations.

In resolving to continue such

HOME FINALLY — It was a long journey for the crew and passengers who arrived from Japan aboard the "Callistratus" Sunday morning to be greeted by the Prince Rupert Fishermen's Co-Op fleet and many well wishers at the Cruise Ship Dock. The $3.4 million vessel, captained by Sid Dickens Jr., was designed by four local fishermen and will catch, process and freeze fish which were formerly caught and processed entirely by foreign vessels fishing off the B.C. coast. The "Callistratus" is the first Canadian-owned freezer trawler to be granted a licence to fish the newly-created 200-mile zone off the B.C. coast. Fish can be caught, processed and frozen within a five-hour period, according to Dickens, but the ship will not be rigged and ready for fishing for a couple of weeks. She will be worked by an 18-man crew and has a capacity of 380 tons of frozen fish. See more

Former longtime resident dies

Funeral services will be held in Nanaimo tomorrow afternoon for a former resident of this area, Walter Herman, who died in the hospital there Friday

When the *Callistratus* arrived in Prince Rupert, it was greeted by a flotilla of boats of all sorts and sizes.

While this rebuilding of the factory space was being organized, the *Callistratus* spent several months anchored in the middle of Prince Rupert Harbour. Margo was still living in Salt Lakes and she came to visit in her clinker-built skiff, the *Cadillac*. She brought a loaf of home-baked bread with her, but the first time found only the oiler and engineer aboard. That was not who she was looking for. The second time she arrived, with another fresh loaf of bread, I was aboard and I was surprised and delighted to discover that she was looking for me. She invited me to dinner at her home and I accepted with alacrity. A day or two later, I arrived at the dock at Salt Lakes in the inflatable Bombardier dinghy from the *Callistratus*, nicknamed the *Black Arrow*. I brought a garbage bag of ice with a bottle of white wine and I never left.

Finally, the installation of the filleting plant began and, after a few months of intense work, the *Callistratus* was ready to go to sea again. The accommodations were expanded to handle a crew of twenty-four people. Margo, our neighbour Lorrie and my sister, Angelika, all worked in that filleting plant.

In the end, the *Callistratus* was able to produce over a million pounds of boneless, skinless hake fillet blocks. Marketing and other issues, however, prevented it from becoming a viable commercial operation. Although the *Callistratus*'s reception in Prince Rupert was very friendly and we had many friends and well wishers, we also had quite a few people opposed to us. The United Fishermen and Allied Workers' Union was hostile to us because they thought we were taking work away from their shore workers. And because the *Callistratus* was a co-op boat, it also had opponents among the handful of big fish companies as well as at the DFO.

One day, we stood in line with other fishermen to get a food herring licence, something we were clearly entitled to. It was handed to us by the clerk who was unaware that he "shouldn't have given it to us" while his boss was away for lunch. That day, however, the government pushed the fastest order ever passed through the Orders in Council Division to specifically prohibit the *Callistratus* from fishing for food herring. This last act so clearly demonstrated that the DFO was discriminating against our vessel that we began a lawsuit against them. The lawsuit had such merit that the DFO eventually felt obliged to purchase the vessel from us at a price just adequate to keep us from going bankrupt.

The *Callistratus* then went through a major refit, at least in part to appease the local shipyards who were quite disgruntled that a big, foreign-built trawler was being purchased by the Canadian government as a research vessel. During that refit, the main trawl winches were hoisted two and a half metres into the air so that a set of new staterooms for the scientific personnel could be installed beneath them. The boat emerged from that refit renamed the *W.E. Ricker.* It roamed the Pacific from Honolulu to Alaska's Dutch Harbour for many years on a wide variety of scientific missions. Margo and I had the amazing experience of attending the memorial service at a decommissioning ceremony in Patricia Bay in October 2017. We were the only people in attendance who had pictures of the vessel's beginnings.

The *Callistratus* brought two big turning points to my life: it started me on my career in marine refrigeration and brought my life partner to me.

Concorde

Stewart Brinton

For a decade, I had been deckhanding on fishing boats from Northern California to Kodiak, Alaska. I had witnessed unfavourable changes. The lucrative nature of the herring roe industry had turbocharged the greed. In the spring of 1978, two cash buyers from Japan flew into Prince Rupert. They were handcuffed to a suitcase stuffed with a million dollars in crisp hundred-dollar bills.

Stewart, like many others in the fishing heyday, saw the rise and fall of the lucrative herring roe industry.

Things were no longer gentlemanly. A blizzard of cash made herring fishing a dangerous game. During an opening on Hornby Island, shotgun blasts were heard as fishermen nervously guarded their gillnets, warding off interlopers. If you got lucky and made a perfect set, you could make a lot of money in a short amount of time. If you got payment from a cash buyer, your profit could be tax free.

The *Vancouver Sun* reported a seiner making a million-dollar set. There was a photo of the captain divvying up the crew share by weighing packets of hundred-dollar bills on a portable scale. A salesman at I.W. Stone Menswear told me that a gillnetter fresh from the herring grounds came into his store, plopped a garbage sack filled with ten grand in cash onto the counter, then gave him a hundred-dollar bill just to watch the garbage sack while he went to the pub and had a beer.

Near the tail end of the 1979 herring season, I was standing by the dock at Cow Bay when a pickup with Manitoba licence plates pulled up lugging a herring punt loaded with gear. The driver asked where the herring grounds were. I pointed in a northerly direction and told him he was too late. His face darkened with disappointment. He was a farmer who had never been to sea before. He figured you just went out there, threw your net in the water and herring jumped into it.

The insanity had a cost. Spring weather is unstable in the North Pacific. The soaring price of herring roe meant a corresponding increase in the cost of licences as well as boats and gear. You could hit it big; you could also go bust. Fishing became high risk and people began pushing the weather to make the openings. A seiner manned by a notable fishing family capsized crossing the Hecate Strait with a hold filled with herring. Church bells in Prince Rupert tolled the loss.

In November 1981, I lost friends in a humongous storm off the west coast of Vancouver Island. The weather satellite had malfunctioned so there was no advance warning as to the ferocity of the impending storm, but old-timers knew better and cautioned everyone to stay in the safety of Ucluelet Harbour. They didn't listen and a bunch of them never made it to the chum salmon opening.

Artists steal time. Commercial fishing was seasonal and, if I collected enough weeks of employment to qualify for UIC (Unemployment Insurance of Canada), it allowed me time in the winter to develop my skills as a writer and musician. And I loved the sea; it was a rollicking, tempestuous medium. Hecate Strait could be glassy smooth at dawn and a wind-whipped maelstrom by afternoon.

A fishing trip meant working long hours. You arose before dawn and retired late in the evening, subsisting on four hours of sleep a day as long as the weather held and the fish kept coming over the rail. A halibut trip could be as long as eight to fourteen days. On a trip to Alaska and back, I once spent a month at sea. I developed a great set of sea legs. After I landed on *terra firma*, it took days before the world stopped swaying beneath my feet.

I loved wooden boats. I remember being in the fo'c'sle, stretched out on my bunk and listening to the creak of wood as the bow rose and dipped in the swell with water rustling along the planking, sending me into a deep sleep cradled by the sea. My romance with wooden fishing boats, however, was fading. The stocks of old-growth, knot-free fir and yellow cedar were becoming hard to acquire and prohibitively expensive. New boats were being built of fibreglass or aluminum. They were called jugs or tin cans and I found them offensive.

Finally, the seiner I had been fishing on, the *Anthony J*, went down in mysterious circumstances in Seymour Narrows, one of the most perilous stretches of water on the British Columbian coast. Two weeks before it went down, I had a premonitory dream and stepped off the boat. I never said anything to anyone about the dream because they would have thought that I was crazy.

It was time to retire from the sea. I had taken a trip to Cuba and their music was so inspirational I bought a saxophone and passionately embraced it. I had a place to play it: a cabin in the alternative community of Salt Lakes situated across the harbour from Prince Rupert. Salt Lakes was a sheltered cove, its entrance signified by a configuration called Horse Head Rocks. The cove was small with the back end leading to a tidal pool that was swimmable, where Salt Lakes got its name.

The Indigenous people the Tsimshian have a long history in Salt Lakes. This was once demonstrated during an extreme spring tide. A boy named Dakota was scouring the beach when he discovered a carved piece of basalt. It had the figures of two salmon and a man with an open mouth. He donated it to the museum. The curator said it was centuries old, a palate for holding paint for ceremonial decoration.

At Salt Lakes, dwellings were scattered along the shoreline. In the fifties, different families in town erected the shacks, intended for summer habitation. The tidal pool had been built up with cement sides and even had a diving board built by volunteers. Charlie Curry arrived with his tug the *CRC* and a pile driver and erected dolphins (pilings tied together at the top) and installed a dock.

By the seventies, Salt Lakes had been forgotten by the townies and began to be inhabited by characters like Blue Jesus, a Russian who remembered listening to Lenin's speeches. He got his nickname from the way he cursed the blue jays that hung around his cabin. In his thick accent, he called them "dem damn blue jaysus."

Blue Jesus died before I arrived at Salt Lakes. Cabins were now filling up with newcomers. In the seventies, the last heyday for logging and fishing, Salt Lakes was populated by a fascinating admixture of former college dropouts as well as graduates, prairie transplants who'd only seen the sea from photographs and renegade longshoremen with drinking problems. Inhabitants half-jokingly referred to this ad hoc community as the Salt Lakes Proving Ground. What were we trying to prove? It was a place where dedicated alcoholics mingled harmoniously with mild-mannered hippy potheads. Everyone at Salt Lakes loomed larger than life. There were communal dinners and bonfires on the beach. There was a quilting group that celebrated marriages and births and made comfort quilts for illness and death. Today, Salt Lakes is abandoned but some of its former members still gather on special occasions and remain in tight communication.

The shacks were on government land and the rent was affordable, that is no rent at all. We cooked with propane stoves, used kerosene or propane

A fishing trip meant long hours—rising before dawn, retiring late in the evening, working as long as the weather held and the fish kept coming over the rail.

for lighting and wood stoves for heat. Firewood was scavenged from loose logs found floating at high tide. You dogged and towed the logs to the beach in front of your cabin. When the tide receded, you chainsawed the logs into usable size for your wood stove. You hoped you hadn't made a greenhorn mistake of towing a hemlock so waterlogged it reeked of teredo worms.

Everyone quickly became nautically inclined because living in Salt Lakes required commuting across the harbour in outboard-powered skiffs. Some of the skiffs were given affectionate names like *Vanessa*, *Emma*, *Stanley* and *La Lune*. My neighbour gave his fibreglass runabout a humorous name, *Kraft Dinner*, because it was fast and easy to fix. I had a seine skiff I called *Turn Over* because I constantly had to beach it and turn it over to patch leaks. It was aggravating. I needed a new skiff.

I was a subscriber to the *National Fisherman* magazine. In one edition, I ran across a photo of a twenty-two-foot aluminum boat that served oil rigs in the Gulf of Mexico. It was a beautiful design with great potential when reduced to sixteen feet. Hans and Margot Elfert lived just down the beach. Hans was a fabricator/welder in aluminum who worked at a shop in town. I showed him the photo, we discussed the price and he agreed to craft it.

A month later, he delivered a fabrication of ingenuity and Germanic exactitude. It was a beautiful replication of the boat in the photo, with the bow pleasingly curved and capped with a roof for storage from the elements. The skiff had sloping lines ending in a transom with a well for the outboard. It was broad beamed and hard chined with a slight keel for sideways stability.

Along each side, Hans had designed continuous seating capped with wooden panels. The seating contained Styrofoam sheets that proofed the skiff against swamping. The skiff could fill with rainwater and the outboard would remain dry and undamaged.

I painted the skiff aquamarine on the outside and grey on the inside. I initially named it the *Cuba Libre* after the nation that gave me such inspiration but then someone else had a better idea and named it the *Concorde*. The name stuck like glue. It became the *Concorde*.

In the engine well, I placed a thirty-five-horsepower Johnson outboard recently refurbished by Dave at Love Electric in Cow Bay. Dave was unique. His parents were members of the Salvation Army but from Dave's appearance you wouldn't have known it. He was a heavy metal rocker with black jeans, black T-shirts and long, straggly black hair. He was an accomplished songwriter and guitarist. His father ran the business and Dave was a mechanic extraordinaire: he had the knack. For his senior shop project, he machined a working miniature Easthope engine. Dave could correctly troubleshoot any problem with an outboard. There was never an overcharge and the work was done properly and promptly. Every waterborne commuter gave a tip of the hat to Love Electric Dave.

Love Electric was a famed spot for mariners—Dave, decked out in black, heavy metal garb, was a mechanic extraordinaire.

I placed an extension onto the handle of the outboard. I wanted to drive the *Concorde* standing up. It gave me great visibility and, at the speed I was going, I had to avoid flotsam, especially half-sunken hemlock logs. Any collision would have thrown me out of the skiff and into very chilly water. Standing up also allowed me to shift my weight and surf. I once thrillingly rode the bow wave of a freighter as it came into the harbour.

Like everyone in Salt Lakes, I had my inclement weather uniform: gumboots (sometimes hip boots) with Helly Hansen trousers fastened in place by shoulder straps and a matching top with hood. Then, I traipsed down to the dock and began bailing rainwater from the *Concorde* with an empty bleach jug cut into a functional shape.

Before I left the dock, I always made sure I had a full tank of gas, a tide chart in my pocket and a working flashlight. After getting lost in the fog one day, I learned to take a compass along and know my headings. I learned an important lesson that day: when lost in fog, left-handers go in a clockwise circle and right-handers go in a counterclockwise circle.

The *Concorde* was delightful, but it was flawed. Aluminum becomes brittle with vibration and the continual pounding just aft of the bow soon created a crack that required patching. I moved into town and gave the *Concorde* to Tsimshian carver Victor Reece and he used it to go back and forth between Prince Rupert and Metlakatla. The *Concorde* was very stable and perfect for his family, with comfortable seating. The *Concorde* could safely handle a lot of cargo. Eventually, the *Concorde* was given to Henry Green, another Tsimshian carver, who used it until it once again developed a crack in the same place; then it was lugged up the beach, turned over and abandoned.

Elora

Lenny Ross

I sailed to the North Coast of British Columbia for all the right reasons! I was young, I was looking for adventure and, most importantly, one of the guiding principles already established in my young life was to always, without fail, never, ever, turn down an opportunity for a boat ride.

This personal mantra served me well when I met the Kristofferson family, Bill, Ruth and their children, Kristie and Kanetta, in Hawaii. I was looking for a sailboat to crew aboard and they were looking for a crew member to join them on their forty-one-foot *Star of Kismet* trimaran. When they asked if I wanted to go on a boat ride, I of course said yes! We would sail the entire Hawaiian chain, from the Big Island to Kuai, before departing for the Queen Charlotte Islands [Haida Gwaii]. I was thrilled to embark on this great adventure but first I had to get out a chart and find out where the heck the Queen Charlottes were!

We had an amazing sailing adventure visiting every Hawaiian island over the next five months. We then sailed north through the trades and eventually into the teeth of several North Pacific gales, until finally we made landfall on the west coast of the Queen Charlotte Islands. In late June of 1975, we carefully navigated our way through Skidegate Narrows to Queen Charlotte City [Daajing Giids].

I had such a great time that now I had a new dream: to build my own trimaran. Bill, a naval architect who had designed the line of Kismet Trimarans, very kindly offered to mentor me through the construction of his newly designed thirty-four footer, even though I had absolutely no building skills or experience at all. We all know the old saying that it takes a village to raise a child. Now, I was going to learn that sometimes it takes a village to build a boat.

Right away, the tiny town warmly welcomed the seafarers who had come all the way from Hawaii to their "city" by the sea. I don't think we could buy a beer in the bar for a month. When people heard that I wanted to build my own boat, the offers of help came in before I even got started. Billy Sahonovitch gave me a floating cabin to live in. The Fournier brothers told me, "Lenny, when you need wood to build this boat of yours, just ask us." And Jimmy LaRose offered a little point of land to build a boatshed on. It had no power, water or parking, was completely treed and on a steep, rocky waterfront (not ideal for boatbuilding), but it was right next

Lenny lived his younger years by the guiding principle of "always, without fail, never, ever turn down an opportunity for a boat ride."

door to the Kristoffersons, who offered not only to help me but also freely gave the warmth and security of being part of their young family when I was so far from home. I turned twenty-one years old with their birthday cake and settled in on making a dream come true.

Building the boatshed was really intimidating when I didn't know which end of a hammer was up. First, I had to learn which end of a chainsaw did the hard work so I could drop a couple of small trees to clear the building site, bring in water with the help of friends on Bahai Hill and have BC Hydro install a pole. Erecting the seven-metre-wide, five-and-a-half-metre-high rigid frames I had made using over-sized, rough-milled lumber and plywood gussets from a Northland shipping container was too much to do alone. Thankfully, my good friend since grade three, Jane Wilde, had arrived in QCC to teach and with her came her partner, Big Bill. Bill offered to give me a hand finishing the massive boatshed jutting out of the forest and hanging over the ocean. It was covered in six-mil plastic and had an array of lights hanging in it so we could work all hours. It became a new navigation beacon on dark nights: the "Hippie Hotel" could be seen for miles out to sea.

With the boatshed underway, I took the Fournier brothers up on their offer of good yellow cedar for boatbuilding. There was no Home Depot for us builders in the North. Again, I had no idea how to do this, but Ray took me up Sleeping Beauty Mountain with his crew early one morning and found a massive yellow cedar that turned out to be over four hundred fifty years old. There were about eighteen metres until there was even a branch, and it stood on a rocky knoll looking over all of Skidegate Channel. It was stunning. Before Ray started cutting it down, I said a little prayer of thanks for such a magnificent being and hugged it firmly for its gift to me. I'm sure Ray was shaking his head as I pulled away from the silvery bark, but then he displayed a logger's skill that was poetry in motion and had the tree on the ground in no time. When it was ready, Ray told me to jump up on his skidder, a crazy logging machine that was part bulldozer, part tow truck and part ATV, with a driver's cage that was not reassuring.

I thought Ray was going to take me along for a ride. Instead, he put me in the driver's seat and said, "Here is the gas, here is the brake, here are the gears, this is the winch, this is the blade, never slow down if the log starts to roll on those steep, sharp logging road turns or the log will roll off the cliff and pull you down with it, instead always give it more gas."

I was appalled. He wanted me to operate this behemoth. My incredulous fear was obvious.

He said, "Dat's what we call a crash course, eh?"

Somehow, Big Bill and I managed to get the logs down to the shore. At the end of the day, we drove down the logging road in Ray's crummy and noticed that we had left a yellow line, like a yellow brick road, out of the forest from dragging the end of the four yellow cedar logs down the hill.

Ray said to us, "Good job, boys, but MacBlo (MacMillan Bloedel) will not be too happy to see you have been stealing their logs when they come to work tomorrow morning. You better get them off the beach by sunrise."

"What do you mean *stealing*?" I yelled as he gunned the engine over another near washout. "I thought you gave us these logs."

"Oh no," he replied. "All these trees belong to MacBlo. I just cut them down, but you plan to take yours home."

Well, he was a well-meaning village helper, but now I was in a pickle. I turned to Billy Sahonovitch, another QCC villager. Billy had a small steel tug with bow teeth and a towing post that he drove so fast he was often called Full Bore Billy. He was a beachcomber who didn't mind working on the shady side of the dock to get his logs. In fact, his other nickname was Capone! I turned to Billy for help and believe it or not he had no trouble getting up at 3 a.m. We pulled those logs off the beach and stashed them in his secret little hidey-hole. And he only wanted me to work as a deckhand for him for a month to pay for his services. No problem. What a great village I lived in!

Now that I had the logs, I had to turn them into number-one-grade, boatbuilding yellow cedar, which, according to Ed Regnery, a local fisherman and boatbuilder, had to be knot free and edge grain only. Luckily, we had a lumber mill in QCC run by Al Porter and his friend Herb. They offered me an even better deal than Billy: rather than working a whole month, I would only have to be their labourer at the mill long enough to cut two bridge beams for each section I wanted milled. My four logs had become sixteen quarter sections; that meant I had to help cut thirty-two beams. I thought that should be quick work. Little did I know that these men, working their 1930s-era mill, didn't work whole days, took lots of holidays for fishing, hunting and drinking, and, while working, stopped for many breaks. I was there over two months! Ah, I was learning about island time and how to really enjoy the support of my village.

And what a village it was. Playing basketball in Skidegate with George and crew. Marching in the hippie kazoo band on Hospital Day with Greg. Early morning chocolate cake, hard as a brick and soaked in condensed milk, at Margaret's Café. Meeting people like Stan, John and Marvin who took me fishing, hunting and scuba diving. All-night dances in the packed Skidegate Community Hall to the heavy rhythms and hard-pounding chords of Skunk Rock. Adventures to Sleeping Beauty Mountain or Rennell Sound with Charlie or out through the narrows on the *Bajo Point* with Art. Commercial salmon fishing with Bill on the little vessel the *Cherokee* (known as the *Rubber Ducky*) and halibut fishing with Keith, a.k.a. Flash. Lending Haida artist Bill Reid my buffer while he finished the first new totem pole in a generation. Building schools, a museum, stores and homes with my mentors. Life was full and busy while I worked to get the money for all the plywood, silicone bronze ring nails and epoxy needed for the next stage of dream building.

Finally, I was ready to get started building my boat. I had so much yellow cedar I made my boatshed's floor out of it and gave away enough for several other small boats and kayaks to be built. But that was okay because I owed the boatbuilding village karmic payback. At last, I could work without needing help, or so I thought. After the huge main hull and two outriggers were built, I asked Bill Kristofferson, "What's next?" He said to go and buy a lot of beer. I didn't get what he meant until he told me that I would need about forty people to pick up and flip the three huge hull constructions and then lift them into position so they could be joined to the deck beams. I was worried, but I shouldn't have been because the village came to my rescue once again. Far more than forty people showed up and they brought food and drink with them. I put on the music and we had a hull-flipping party with many friends!

One friend who was there before there were any parties was the amazing Butterfly Ron. Fly was always there for me. He would end his nocturnal wanderings by stopping by my floathouse to get me up. He would start up the airtight stove and break the ice in the bucket to boil my tea while he told me to "Get up! Get up, Captain Ross! It's time to get to work on your dream boat!" He was the epitome of a character. *Zen and the Art of Motorcycle Maintenance* personified. A massive head of bushy hair under his bamboo conical hat that kept the rain from rusting the many zippers on his leather jacket. We would sip tea, look at the boat plans on the wall and dream of tight sails dancing over shining seas. Later, he often slept in my boatshed while working on his fifteen-foot open-sailing dory. Or he would use the boatshed to dry his kelp harvest. Nothing like drying seaweed to add to the ambience of a boatshed. Over the long four years of building, whenever he was there, he always asked how he could help and he never failed to leave without an encouraging word to keep working: "Your dream is coming true!"

Elora, named for the small town near where Lenny was born, provided a safe and cozy home to Lenny and Carmen for several years.

Building the boat became much more than building a boat. There were so many people who helped me I can't mention them all, but I am thankful for them all! Then I met Carmen, the love of my life and still my best friend. We got married by the sea at the Kristoffersons'. Art and Annie took pictures of that perfect party. We raised our awesome boat dog, Maggie, and then raised our incredible boat kid, Daniel. I learned the skills of a carpenter and how to work hard, respect others and be a good man from Greg Martin, Albert

Myshrall, Al Houdek and Faraj Behbehani. I discovered a way to live my life from the Kristoffersons, one centred around family, filled with adventure and grounded in nature. With the love and support of a whole community of generous souls, I learned to be appreciative of how I could accomplish more than I can dream of.

We launched the boat and had another beach party. Carmen named her the *Elora* after a small town near where I was born, a town named after an English tea clipper that sailed the high seas and that was named after the Buddhist, Hindu and Jain Ellora Caves in India. After living in boatsheds, float homes and tiny cabins, we found living aboard to be both comfortable and thrilling. I loved how living on the boat brought us so close to nature. Seabirds, seals and sea lions were our companions. Sometimes, a dolphin or a whale crossed our bows. Checking the weather every day became a vital part of our daily routine. We sailed with Butterfly Ron, the "mayor" of Juan Perez Sound, who was an excellent sailor.
Our dream turned into a reality that was beyond our expectations when we explored the amazing north pacific archipelago that would become the world famous Gwaii Haanas National Park Reserve. Bathing at Hotspring Island [G̲andll K'in Gwaay.yaay]. Enjoying abalone, mussel and scallop feasts on the Bischof Islands. Hunkering down as the winds howled above us and Heron and Daniel played on the wing berth in Echo Bay. Visiting Lon and Susan in Swan Bay. Eating lush salads from Susan's garden with fresh salmon caught on the way into Rose Harbour. The *Elora* was our safe and cozy home from Queen Charlotte City to Victoria for several years.

I learned many lessons in Haida Gwaii that I try to pass onto others, just as so many shared their wisdom with me. I went back to school and became an environmental and Indigenous-knowledge teacher. I spent thirty years taking students to the seashore so that they could explore, paddle canoes, sail and learn about the nature and cultures of our amazing place here on the coast. Our son, Daniel, who enjoys surfing and replenishing his spirit by the ocean, carries on a love of the sea. Recently, I got to help him and his wife build their dream, a waterfront cottage that they call Elora Oceanside Retreat. Now, I spend my time there or volunteering at Swan Lake Christmas Hill Nature Sanctuary, where I'm contributing to the positive village work of building community and supporting dreamers.

And I still never, ever turn down a boat ride.

La Lune

Sébastien Liénard-Boisjoli

The nine years that I spent in Prince Rupert amounted to nearly a decade of happiness. I arrived in Prince Rupert by train in January 1973 and left by car in August 1981.

Like many whom I befriended, I was in my twenties, free and adventurous. Although I came from an island, Montreal, boats had very little meaning to me. As a teenager, I did have dreams of sailing around the world but that never happened. Just a pipe dream. I was twenty-three years old when I arrived in Prince Rupert and it was only a couple of years later, living at Function Junction on the dock, that owning a boat became a possibility. It couldn't be a very large one because I didn't have much money and I didn't know much about boating. This would be just a small boat for pleasure.

One day, the opportunity came to buy a small, flat-bottomed plywood rowboat, which measured about ten feet from bow to stern and had

Sébastien and friend Jane perform an impromptu concert on the dock for Linda.

a beam of about four feet. It was in pretty good shape. I undertook to turn it into a sailboat, a catboat that would have one mast near the bow and a simple, triangular sail. I had to build a daggerboard and a daggerboard well, install the mast and rigging, and make a canvas sail. Although I was handy and unafraid of such a project, I was helped by other Gumbooters who themselves had big boats, skiffs or dinghies. Paul Manson, Bruce Anderson and Bill Edbrooke were always supportive and helpful. The daggerboard well was especially challenging but help with design and fibreglass was always close and available.

Sébastien found a ten-foot flat-bottomed rowboat, converted it into a sailboat and christened it *La Lune*.

I named my boat the *La Lune*. I painted the name on the bow in such a way that you could only read it reflected in the water. After all, you can only see the moon when the sun's light bounces off it.

Once it was all done, I quickly learned to handle the sailboat with the basics of sailing. I enjoyed sailing it, often solo, and sometimes took a Gumboot Girl for a sail in the harbour in fair weather. A few times, I took James to Salt Lakes for the day. Pretty tame adventures.

However, there was one outing that I will never forget. It was New Year's Eve, 1977, at 11:30 p.m. In the past, I had always made a point of recording in a diary where I was at the very beginning of each year. That year, I decided on something poetically original: to row *La Lune* to the middle of the harbour by myself and, at midnight, light my kerosene lantern and hang it up at midmast. All went well at first, but fifteen minutes into 1978, there were spotlights on my boat and five fishing boats surrounded me, screaming, "What the hell are you doing? Are you okay?" I sheepishly explained what I was doing, which they could not in a million years understand. Eventually, I was "encouraged" to row back and one of the fishing boats escorted me to the Function Junction dock. I was very surprised to see how many fishermen were out there, aware of the harbour and noting atypical activities at odd times. Even though I was safe with a windless night, I was impressed to learn how many eyes were aware in the harbour, no matter when.

In the end, when Function Junction had to be torn down and I decided to build a house on leased land in Crippen Cove, Linda Gibbs bought the *La Lune*. I was pleasantly surprised to see a photograph of her sailing it in the harbour when I read *Gumboot Girls*.

Function Junction was a communal building, and the dock was used by many to access the community.

Margarita the Coffin

Paul Manson

You could hear them for a good minute before they showed up as dark specks against a darkening grey sky. The geese would fly southward every autumn, closely following British Columbia's rugged coastline, flock after flock flying in high elevation, in roughly V-shaped formations, letting their presence be known with non-stop squawking. It was a sight to behold! I thought, *A great time for an ocean adventure!*

My new girlfriend, Lorrie, and I had gotten together a few weeks before, both of us relatively new arrivals to Prince Rupert. Lorrie had recently moved out to the coast from northern Saskatchewan after finishing high school. I had arrived a couple of years earlier. Having grown up in downtown New York, I was blown away by the raw, majestic beauty and unbridled freedom of the North Coast.

Paul's *Margarita* was just fourteen feet long and maxed out at three knots.

When I arrived in Prince Rupert, my friend John Cross had generously offered to let me stay at his beachfront cabin in Salt Lakes, across the harbour from the town, and it had been an intense period for me of picking up the skills of seaside country living: learning about kerosene lamps and chainsaws; using the tides to collect and move logs that had escaped from the floating booms of the local logging industry, and then cutting and splitting the wood on the beach for firewood; building woodsheds; and capturing rain or creek water for year-round use. As Salt Lakes was only accessible by boat, the community of twenty or so residents there had a fleet of small wooden and aluminum boats powered by outboard motors to travel back and forth to town.

By that time, I had been commercial fishing for a few years, so the lifestyle at Salt Lakes blended well with my growing familiarity with boats. In the fishing off-season, I had gotten work at local shipyards and had helped to build several commercial fishing boats out of fibreglass.

I was anxious to show Lorrie the beauty of the North Coast, outside the confines of Prince Rupert's visually land-bound harbour, but I wanted to pick a great destination. Ben Russett and his family, formerly my neighbours in Salt Lakes, had moved up to Georgetown Mills a few months before and they offered to let me use their home, an old house once occupied by the mill manager, while they were in town for a few days. The water-powered sawmill at Georgetown had been built in 1875, a hundred years earlier, but had been abandoned for quite some time. In its day, it was the largest water-powered sawmill on the North Coast and supplied timber to the Yukon during the Klondike Gold Rush. When the city of Prince Rupert, twenty-four kilometres to the south, was incorporated in 1910, Georgetown Mills had a resurgence of business.

The year before, Richard Fish, a close friend and fishing partner, had taken me up to Georgetown on his thirty-six-foot salmon-fishing boat, the *Norah Flynn*. The water flumes and gateways that had powered the mill were still visible, but the entire mill and townsite, now a ghost town, were well on their way to being recaptured by the North Coast's rainforest. It was the sort of place where the tools of the trade had been open-end wrenches just over a metre long, each weighing about twenty-three kilograms, and slow-moving, circular saw blades, one-by-one-and-a-half metres across. Other than the Russett family, no one lived within kilometres of it. So, Georgetown it was.

The boat that we would use for the trip was the *Margarita the Coffin*, about fourteen feet long and which made an honest three nautical miles per hour if the wind and tide were in favour. The boat was one of the last of its class, with a wooden lapstrake of Norwegian design and a lovely sheer. It was a great sea boat. It had been built long before outboards made their appearance and was designed to be powered by oars. As it was well past its prime when I acquired it, due to the challenges of repairing wooden boats of lapstrake design, I had applied my new fibreglassing skills to give it a second life. Having successfully weathered its sea tests crossing the harbour numerous times in wild weather, I was quite confident in its performance out in open water. A friend had given me a small gaff sailing rig that I thought would fit well on the boat. I had never sailed before but figured there couldn't be much to it.

The outboard chosen for the trip was not really a choice. I had secured the exclusive franchise to sell Seagull outboard engines for the Prince Rupert region the year before. Geoff Potter, another neighbour who had just opened Prince Rupert's first health-food store, Ambrosia Foods, let me

Designed to be powered by oars, the *Margarita* was given a second life with a fibreglass hull and new Seagull outboard.

display one of the outboard motors on the wall of his store. I was never sure if people were simply confused by the idea of buying an outboard motor from a health-food store, but in any event, the Seagull outboards turned out not to be popular at all, so I had a couple of them hanging around.

With the question of destination settled, Lorrie and I set about provisioning and packing for the sea voyage. Not least of the stores for the trip was a large bottle of Lambs Navy Rum. I figured that one never knew when a fifth of rum might come in handy.

A day or so later, we cast off, taking the falling tide out through Metlakatla Pass to the open waters of Chatham Sound and Dixon Entrance. As we came out from behind Tugwell Island, in the far distance we could see the mountains on Prince of Wales Island, the southernmost point on the Alaskan Panhandle. Japan was just over the horizon!

All was well for the first hour or so, although a stiff southeast wind was picking up, with small whitecaps occasionally sloshing into the boat. The gaff sail performed okay but didn't really move the boat any faster than the outboard would have. A couple of hours in, bucking a falling tide, we were still well south of our destination.

With the temperature dropping, I made an executive decision and cracked open the bottle of rum. Against the chilly temperature and stiff breeze, it felt and tasted good. *Well*, I thought, *if some is good, more is better!* As the level of rum in the bottle dropped, I began to really enjoy the movement of the boat. I began singing an old sea shanty about a sinking pirate ship caught in a storm that I had learned as a kid but could only remember the first verse and the chorus, so I sang them both a few times. The odd lone seagull would swoop down or circle for a moment to take in the sight.

We were about halfway there and could see the headland of Georgetown Bay in the distance. However, we weren't going very fast and with an early dusk at that time of year, I was a little worried about arriving there before nightfall. Lorrie was not fond of rum but didn't seem too concerned about my enhanced sense of appreciation for the voyage, so when the level of rum in the bottle dropped below half, it wasn't a hard decision to do my duty and polish it off.

Eventually, we rounded the southern point of land and headed into Georgetown Bay. Although I had been there before with Richard, I was not familiar with the channel at the head of the bay that lead to the dock. Fortunately, being reasonably well practised in the art of functional inebriation, I was able to steer the skiff up the channel, through the shoals exposed by the fallen tide, safely to the dock. I slipped a mooring line onto the dock, staggered out of the boat and promptly passed out.

And there I would have lain, perhaps into the hereafter, with what was left of my body heat quickly dissipating into the chilly, gathering dusk, were it not for the goodness of Lorrie! She left me on the dock and ran up to the old house on the bluff that we were to occupy. In the house, there was a wood-stove heater made from a 170-litre oil drum. Using her new skills from living off-grid in Salt Lakes, she quickly got a rip-roaring fire going. She then returned to the dock and either dragged or prodded me up the embankment to the house, where I warmed up and survived to enjoy a memorable hangover the next day. So, I didn't make it to the hereafter on that trip after all!

Now, fifty years later, after co-raising our two wonderful children, Elisha and Ezra, and watching two amazing grandchildren, Malcolm and Moss, grow up, Lorrie and I remain friends and neighbours living in Powell River. In fact, just before starting to write this story this morning, we enjoyed pancakes made by ten-year-old Malcolm, while his brand new sister Moss (six months old today!) practised chewing on a carrot.

Marvellous Pelican

Rick Sobel

It started in Moss Landing, California, a small fishing village on Monterey Bay. I was hanging out there doing a research project for university and I met a group of guys from the Marvel Boat Farm, a boatbuilding commune. They had a lot of projects on the go to pay the rent, one of which was constructing a seventeen-foot, bowed-transom sailing scow, with lines taken from a twelve-foot San Francisco Bay Pelican pram. I acquired this unfinished hull and was pleased to find that it had been expertly planked with Douglas fir. A friend helped me move and finish it, including rigging it with a junk sail. Then we decided on an adventure: north to Alaska! We towed the boat to Washington state and sailed it from there into BC waters.

I was so overwhelmed by the natural beauty and the great people I was meeting that I decided to stay and immigrate. In 1971, it was easy to make money. Sailing around, I met a wonderful couple on a unique small

Rick's first encounter with the Hecate Strait was during an ambitious sailing adventure from Monterey Bay, California, to Alaska.

Wooden boat building was still very active in Prince Rupert. Rick was among those who took it up, renting a shed in Dodge Cove.

sailboat and we made plans to sail to the Queen Charlotte Islands [Haida Gwaii] the following spring.

Once headed north, we found safe anchorages every night. After a month or so, we arrived at a jumpoff for crossing Hecate Strait, a body of water named for the daughter of hell. We had gained confidence on the long haul north, but this was open water and an overnight crossing. I landed in Queen Charlotte City [Daajing Giids] the next day to a round of applause for my bravado. Thus began the legend of the *Marvellous Pelican*, the small boat that crossed the Hecate Strait. As if this was not enough, I took out the *Pelican* and a buddy took a small boat called the *Nid*. We went through the ditch, as the Skidegate Channel was sometimes called, and we found ourselves in the big yard of the open Pacific. We had many adventures on our way south to Anthony Island [Skungwai] and up the east side to all the hippie encampments and abandoned Haida village sites.

As fall came on, I decided to go back across the Hecate to Prince Rupert. Miscalculation caused me to be bounced in the strait for seventy-two hours! It was not life threatening, but I was at its mercy! I was at least a week getting to Rupert, looking for both work and pleasure. In 1972, Prince Rupert had lots of both, so much that I stayed for thirty years.

I crossed the strait many times in that small boat after that and it taught me to be a good sailor and a crackerjack deckhand. On a night

Rick and the *Marvellous Pelican* crossed the Hecate Strait many times over the years.

near Langara Island [Kiis G̱waay], hosting a sit-down dinner for five, I got the idea that I needed a larger boat. So, in either 1978 or 1979, I quit a rewarding job and spent my saved wages on lumber. Wooden boatbuilding was still very active in Prince Rupert and boatbuilding dreams could come true. I rented a shed in Dodge Cove and lots of friends showed up to help me on my way. I eventually ended up with a vessel that I named the *Rupert Pelican* and made it my home for many years.

The land of rainbows made dreams come true for me.

Mud Puppy

Bill Edbrooke

We arrived in Prince Rupert in February with a name and a phone number scrawled on a notepad. Jan helped us settle in and find a place to live. Shelley, our dog Barney, all our possessions and I were crammed into our other love, the 1954 Ford sedan we brought from the Okanagan. Rupert promised jobs, money and adventure. The first two were delivered in spades. We worked, saved, took off to Mexico the next winter and returned four months later. Open to all possibilities and hungry for the third promise, we decided to move across the harbour when the opportunity presented itself. Crippen Cove is a muddy bay about one nautical mile from the co-op dock. We were now the new caretakers of the little yellow Harding house on the point. We moved north to work, but as soon as we could we retired! No power or telephone, but who cared? We had money, friends, delicious seafood and enough projects to keep us busy: the outhouse, the woodshed and a sauna.

Bill and Shelley arrived in Prince Rupert in February, and quickly realized that they needed a boat.

In the end, practicality won out in the form of an aluminum skiff and a twenty-horsepower outboard.

I knew very little about boats and boating. I had been to Crippen a couple of times and Salt Lakes, too, but always with somebody else. We learned from our friends' examples. They helped us get to and from town and advised us of everything we would need. Between the Fisherman's Supply and the thrift shop, we were soon supplied with gumboots, rain gear, floater coats and whatever else was required for life on the water.

Of course, we needed a boat. That was when the *Mud Puppy* came into our lives. I don't remember what I paid for it, if anything. Our neighbour Geoff had it, he didn't need it, so I took it over. It was a nineteen-foot plywood mini cruiser with a 5-7-horsepower, single-cylinder Easthope engine that had probably come out of a small river gillnetter. The boat became my new obsession. I lost interest in the Ford and eventually traded it for a six-horsepower outboard motor. I was shocked when I saw the car a couple of days later sporting a new two-tone, cream-and-powder-blue paint job. The new owner's partner was an artist and had carefully painted it with fine brushes from the hardware store.

Actually, the Ford and the Easthope had a lot in common. Both were old fashioned, out of date and very cool. I applied the skills I had learned troubleshooting and caring for the car to the boat. Easthope parts were still available from Steveston; soon, the *Mud Puppy* was fairly reliable.

The *poof, poof* sound was like a heartbeat. I believe it idled at about the speed of my current resting pulse, around seventy revolutions per minute. It only needed three things: spark, gas and cooling water. Starting it was a trip. First, a series of checks and adjustments: open the gas valve, the drip oiler, the ignition and a couple of other things I can't remember. Then sit spread-eagle with the flywheel between the knees. Grab the flywheel with both hands and ease it over to the left. The first trick was to give it a little extra push at the right moment as it passed the compression stroke to create enough momentum so it would fire again on the next revolution and keep going. This usually involved several tries and maybe some

With a few replacement parts, new handrails and a paint job, the *Mud Puppy* was a reliable and comfortable vessel.

backfiring on a cantankerous day. And maybe some sweet talk followed by some cursing, depending on how it was going. The second trick was a little more difficult: to try to keep the grease and oil from covering my hands and clothes. (Tip: never wear a long, dangling scarf when attempting to start an Easthope.)

Our top speed was about five knots, slow enough that when Barney, our lab (and first baby), fell overboard unnoticed, he was able to just about keep up until I saw him dog-paddling furiously beside the boat.

Pretty soon, I got comfortable taking the *Mud Puppy* all around the harbour, to Salt Lakes, Dodge Cove and, of course, back and forth to town. It was slow but stable for such a small boat. In a wind-driven swell, the Easthope would slow down as it climbed the wave and speed up as it slid down into the trough. We should have been scared but we weren't. It died once, in the dark on the way home to Crippen. A gigantic Rivtow tug rescued us and towed us back to the co-op dock. Another time, completely disoriented and lost in the fog, we saw a strange glow that appeared to be moving on the horizon. We thought we were seeing a UFO, but it was just a mast light on a sailboat, anchored and waiting for the fog to lift.

Eventually, the boat was pretty tiddly, with new bottom paint, new canvas, handrails and even a V-shaped berth and small wood stove. A trip farther afield was in order, so after much preparation, we set out for

Serpentine Inlet on Porcher Island, with stops at Hunt's Inlet, Oona River and Billy Bay. That trip was the highlight of our time with the *Mud Puppy*.

Money was running low; we needed to get back to work in town. The mud and the tide were a daily challenge at Crippen. Crippen Cove is a shallow bay that dries out for about fifty metres, revealing a vast, gooey barrier between us and the boat out on the mooring. Tide's up: no problem. Low tide was a challenge. The "clothesline" acted much like the laundry version, except it was connected to a small raft maybe thirty metres out in the chuck. Instead of hanging up clothing, you pulled a small skiff out to deep water. If it floated, you pulled the skiff to the water's edge, trudged out through the mud and you were on your way. Fun! Often, the end of the clothesline would be high and dry or nearly so, necessitating a race against the tide. You'd have to drag a skiff through the mud, sometimes after removing the outboard motor, then back to the dock, back to the skiff, to water deep enough to float. And don't forget the outboard. Yikes!

The challenge of the shallow bay necessitated the acquisition of a fleet of boats: a nine-foot Davidson skiff for the clothesline and a twelve-foot Davidson with the six horse for beachcombing firewood. Practicality was slowly winning out, but we were still enjoying the *Mud Puppy*. Our excursions became less frequent but always fun: crabbing and fishing in Venn Passage or out to Tugwell Island for a picnic. Rupert on a sunny day is so shiny and gorgeous. In those days, you could land anywhere and never see a No Trespassing sign. More likely, you'd be invited in for tea.

When we went back to work, living full time in Crippen became too difficult for us. We took an apartment in town and spent weekends across the harbour. Looking back, I realize we were living through the end of an era. When we arrived in Rupert, there were still a couple of gillnetters running twin-cylinder Easthope engines. Beautiful wooden fishboats were still being built in the boatsheds of Dodge Cove. Now, most of the places we worked at are gone, including the Sunnyside and Port Essington canneries on the Skeena River. The area was a magnet for young people from all over Canada and the world. I feel very lucky to have participated in that part of Prince Rupert's history and to have made so many good friendships that I cherish to this day.

Eventually, we gave up the *Mud Puppy* and passed it on. Practical modernity arrived in the form of a fourteen-foot welded-aluminum skiff from Marinex in Cow Bay. Gino, the owner and master builder of large herring skiffs and large powerboats, also built smaller skiffs to the same high standards. He adapted Glen-L patterns for plywood to aluminum, creating tough, fast, safe boats with twenty-horse outboards that were ideal commuters for zipping back and forth to Crippen. By that time, we were building a small house and needed something capable of towing building materials for our new project.

As much as I loved the romance of the *Mud Puppy*, I also enjoyed the speed and convenience of bombing around in my new toy. A twenty-minute trip became five, skipping from wave top to wave top. Our new skiff was practical and indestructible, but it never had a name.

Nid and *Cymbeline*

Illtyd Perkins

I came to British Columbia from England in 1968 to teach in the English department of the University of Victoria. I had no notion where or what British Columbia was, except perhaps a hazy notion that it might somehow be associated with South America. It is hard to exaggerate the arrogant insularity of a young and ignorant English colonist.

Upon moving to BC from England, Illtyd immediately realized that he would need a boat to properly explore his new home.

Flying from the Vancouver airport to Patricia Bay, I was astounded to see the vast archipelago of passages and islands spread out below. My first thought in this new and unknown land was, *I'll need a boat.* I had no experience of the sea or boats (other than rowing in a crewed eight on the Thames at Chiswick), but in a very short time I found an old twenty-two-foot converted lifeboat moored at West Bay Marina. Tides? Currents? Charts? Weather forecasts? I learned a lot, but I sank that boat at the dock with a lot of University of Victoria library books on board.

After some pottering around Southern Vancouver Island in the *Gimli*, a slightly larger powerboat, reaching the Queen Charlotte Islands [Haida Gwaii] seemed possible. But the two barriers of Queen Charlotte Sound and the fearsome Hecate Strait kept me from reaching the goal.

One bright January day, winter cruising with my companion, Joanne Hemmingsen, we arrived at the western end of Hole in the Wall, near Quadra Island, too early to go through the rapids. Forced to wait for slack water, we threw our anchor overboard and turned off the engine. Suddenly, we could hear birds all around us and water gently slapping against the hull. A week later, we headed south and began searching for a sailboat.

Sailboats, licence-buyback fishboats to convert; we looked at everything. Finally, in Seattle we found a US Navy minesweeper in a dry dock that had been sent into salvage in the middle of a refit. Its captain's gig, a twenty-six-foot whaleboat planked with yellow cedar and fastened with non-magnetic silicon bronze screws, had just had five of its six waterline planks replaced. The price was $500. It also had a massive Buda diesel amidships, which we disposed of for scrap. A few days later, a *War of the Worlds*-sized crane reached over two military vessels, picked up the gig and laid it onto our rented flatbed truck. We headed off to a boatyard on Lake Union and started converting it to a sailboat.

Four months later, we sailed our new gaff cutter, the *Nid*—with all six planks in place, a concrete fin keel bolted on, a varnished cabin with galley and table and bunk, and even baggywrinkle on the stays (but no engine)—back to Tsehum Harbour in Sidney. Pat and Hubert Havelaar, friends from Shawnigan Lake, crossed and went to Victoria with us. They had been so excited when we found the gig that they came down to Seattle and bought the sister gig, a crew whaleboat in rougher shape. Five planks were still missing but they gave it an entire wineglass shape in ferrocement and a higher cabin. They named it the *Arché*.

In July, we abandoned everything including our car, spent our last hundred dollars on food supplies (saving twenty-five cents for the famous emergency phone call) and headed north. Anchored at Newcastle Island [Saysutshun], we heard someone else sail in alongside us and chuck an anchor overboard the *Marvellous Pelican*, a small, blunt-nosed, flat-bottomed, junk-rigged scow. A second head popped out from under a tarp, and then a third, and then a child! To our complete astonishment, there were three adults and a nine-year-old on that sixteen-foot boat: Rick Sobel and his friends Beau, Wanda and Gabby.

The *Nid* was a former US Navy minesweeper, purchased for $500 and converted into a sailboat over four months.

Before the summer was over, the *Nid* suffered an almost-terminal fire at the dock at Kelsey Bay caused by a carelessly stored can of gas, a propane refrigerator and the swell of a passing vessel. We spent weeks dejectedly scraping charcoal off our beautiful cabin varnish and mourning our one tin of marmalade. Months later, we collected twenty dollars' worth of beer bottles in an abandoned logging camp (at twenty-five cents a dozen!) and turned them in for new food supplies when we finally got to Port Hardy.

After tree planting in Seymour Inlet, we sailed across Queen Charlotte Strait to Blunden Harbour, where we were weathered in for seven weeks during the fierce winter of 1971. When the gales let up for a day in mid-January, we made the coldest sail of our lives: seventeen nautical miles along Queen Charlotte Strait, taking half-hour turns in the open cockpit. Then, the *Nid* got iced in again in Wells Passage. Word got around of newcomers in the area; a skiff came by while we waited for slack tide, and on the strength of having done the conversion on the *Nid*, I was offered a job renovating a sixty-foot powerboat in Owen Lane's Turnbull Cove logging camp, which also included a small house on a log float where we could tie up the *Nid* for the remainder of the winter. We saved enough money to buy supplies and a small outboard motor, a British Seagull, surely one of the noisiest and dirtiest outboards ever made.

In the spring of 1972, we set north again. On the way, we stopped briefly at Telegraph Cove. Our log entry for May 15 reads: "Guess who we found under the *Pelican* putting gumwood on the keel." Travelling in the same direction, people inevitably cross paths. We met Richard and the *Pelican* in Port McNeill, Bella Bella, Cougar Bay near Klemtu, Butedale, Port Stephens, Colby Bay and Abalone Bay.

Our plan was to cross the Hecate Strait from Larsen Harbour on the north end of Banks Island to Skidegate Channel and Queen Charlotte City [Daajing Giids]. When Rick crossed over, we diverted to Prince Rupert, then followed on a week later. We finally found the *Pelican* tied up at the Queen Charlotte government dock on Sunday, July 16.

By the time we arrived, Rick had already made friends and found a crew for the west coast trip. We took Rick's new crewmate Tom Forge, an

One of the catamaran's greatest tricks was its ability to sit comfortably on any beach.

absolutely inexperienced English visitor, out with us for a week while Richard spent the weekend with another friend. On the last day of July, we found Richard waiting in Armentieres Channel and we transferred Tom from our twenty-six foot *Nid* to Rick's sixteen-foot *Pelican*. At the beginning of August, the *Pelican* and the *Nid* headed out of Skidegate Channel and began exploring north up Graham Island and then south along the west coast of Moresby Island. Because both boats only carried small, easily swamped emergency outboards, we cautiously worked the winds and tried to avoid calms and fog. We met fishing boats and a fisheries patrol boat in Kaisun, ate salmon and deer, and often waited days for a sailing breeze.

While the *Pelican* whooshed into Tasu Harbour on huge swells, the *Nid* carried on exploring down the coast. The *Pelican* reappeared when we reached the south end of Moresby and we anchored together south of Anthony Island [Skungwai], on the edge of the ocean. As we walked among ancient spirits in the most amazing place we had ever been, a helicopter landed on the beach. Visitors from Tasu Mines rushed about with cameras for ten minutes and then were gone.

The trip round Moresby took more than two months. By early October, we had reached Cumshewa Inlet, where we waited out multiple gales. After several days of these gales, Richard decided to catch the one day of northwest wind in the forecast. On Thanksgiving Day, we watched the *Pelican* sail out of sight past Kingui Island. Two days later, on October 11, we came twenty-nine nautical miles around Sandspit Bar, with a flat, calm sea and a glorious twelve-knot breeze, into Skidegate Channel and then on to Queen Charlotte City against the tide.

We recall in later years glancing around the tables at Margaret's Café at the beginning of September to see who had outstayed the summer. Since we didn't arrive until mid-October, we were grateful for the friendliness of other dock dwellers: the Watmoughs, Art Dirk, Al Porter, Rags, Lyn Pinkerton and John Lockwood. Karl Kulesha tentatively lent us his Stihl 08 S chainsaw so we could buck up a winter's firewood log out at Lina Island. The hospital administrator, Dr. Hugh McGuire, who was on the Charlottes to pilot an innovative tele-medicine project, offered me a job building a roof over the doctor's trailer.

One of the wonderful things about the Charlottes was that if you had enough determination to figure out how to do the work, you could get a job. Thank you to the Canadian government in that first winter for the Local Initiatives Program (LIP). In the winter of 1973, I helped Dean Nomura set up and paint the walls in his dental office. Eventually, both Joanne and I went to work for Dean as office staff. We took turns being the receptionist and the dental assistant. There is a wonderful photo somewhere of the very first day of Dean's practice, with an inexpressibly brave Reverend Bob Henderson opening his mouth to Dean with an extremely bearded Illtyd sitting by passing dental tools.

For five glorious years, we sailed every summer, for two to five months. By late fall every year, we would be back in QCC looking for a job, buying new rubber boots and restocking the food cupboard with a bulk order from Canasoy in Vancouver. Good friends, potluck dinners, dances and Greg Martin's weekly race home to see *Monty Python's Flying Circus* made dark winters enjoyable.

In 1973, after another summer circumnavigating Moresby, I decided I wanted to build a forty-foot Wharram catamaran. Del Fowler had brought one of the World War II office buildings over from Alliford Bay and dragged it up on to the beach next to his and Fran's house in QCC. We worked for weeks to take out all the interior office walls until the building was one huge, draughty, eighteen-by-twelve-metre workshop with a tiny sleeping attic on the seaside that we moved into. To finance the catamaran, we had to sell the *Nid*, which was extremely painful. When winter came, on stormy nights, even after it was no longer ours, one of us would drive down to the dock to check the lines on the *Nid*.

Late in 1973, two keels were laid down and I began to build. The *Cymbeline* was launched in the fall of 1974 with the help of many friends but narrowly avoided disaster when it slid off one of the two hull ramps. Fortunately, with deep breaths all around, the tide was very high and the *Cymbeline* landed nicely in the water. One of the *Cymbeline*'s greatest tricks was its ability to sit comfortably on any beach. By March 1975, the *Cymbeline* was rigged and in July we left again for the west coast.

For the *Cymbeline*'s first summer, we headed up the west coast of Graham Island, carrying a different small outboard, and crossed Dixon Entrance to Baranof Island in Alaska. We sailed up the outside coast of Baranof and Chichagof islands, eventually turning in Cross Sound to Glacier Bay. Seeing trees emerge from bare rocks and then become a full forest eighty kilometres down the pathway of the receding glacier gave us a great insight: every kilometre represented one year of the regenerating forest!

We were grateful to Dr. Bayla Schecter, who wired fifty dollars to the only bank in Juneau for us to buy enough emergency outboard gas to return to Prince Rupert. After five years and a trip down the east coast of Moresby to Vancouver Island, it was clear that we were beginning to settle in. Between us, besides construction, dentistry and LIP projects, we worked for Bayla Schecter and Russ Ellison's medical practice, spent a winter as local coordinator for the Terrace Community College and as replacement First Aid attendant in Dinan Bay and Rennell Sound. Either we were going to buy property, build a career and settle down, or we were going to go offshore in the *Cymbeline*. We visited Richard in Dodge Cove where there was a boathouse for sale, but we decided that after a six-year apprenticeship among the wild rocks of the North Coast, we would never be quite as ready to sail offshore again as we were right then.

One morning in May 1977, having said goodbye to Fran Fowler the night before, we were busy untying the *Cymbeline*'s lines to the QCC dock when an acquaintance wandered by. He said, "You are leaving now? Just like that?" And we were. No goals announced, no promises made: we were heading south. And we left.

From Vi Halsey's column "Rennell Sounds" in the *Queen Charlotte Observer* in June 1978: "From across the miles came a postcard from Joanne Hemmingsen. Joanne was First Aid attendant here and now lives in Mexico. Illtyd is teaching English there. They are both learning Spanish and are very happy enjoying the sun. We understand they get the *Observer* and are still keen and interested in the Islands. All in camp send their greetings."

Illtyd wishes to thank Joanne, his partner in life and so much else, including the writing of this story.

Norah Flynn

For Richard Fish (1944–2018)

written by Paul Manson

The Canadian Coast Guard's radio frequency for marine weather was crackling with static as they identified the station using a phonctic call sign. "This is Bull Harbour Coast Guard Radio—Whiskey Papa Hotel India. Following is the marine forecast for Lower Hecate Strait and Queen Charlotte Sound. Winds are expected to be ten to fifteen knots from the northwest this evening and through the night, shifting to light easterlies by the morning."

Richard Fish and I were anchored up in his thirty-six-foot salmon gillnetter, the *Norah Flynn*, in a small bay on the seaward side of Princess

Richard bought his boat, the *Norah Flynn*, in Vancouver in 1974.

Royal Island, one of the loneliest places on British Columbia's remote central coast. It was the middle of herring season in February 1987 and we were waiting to hear from the federal Department of Fisheries and Oceans (DFO) as to when and where the next twenty-four-hour roe herring fishery opening would be scheduled. Over the course of the season, the DFO would monitor the spawn and egg maturity of the schools of herring congregating in the inshore spawning areas and try to schedule a fishery for optimum quality of the roe. Little advance notice would typically be given by the DFO for the fishing openings and, once announced, there would be a mad rush by the fleet of a couple hundred similarly sized boats to reach the designated area in time.

A big part of the risk assessment was whether to tempt fate by heading out into stormy weather to make an opening, but we always did anyway. Feast or famine: if we arrived at the opening in time, we would each

The *Norah Flynn* was a solid vessel, but the wheelhouse needed a rebuild after a particularly violent thrashing in stormy seas.

make up to $1,000 per hour. But if we didn't, we headed home with nothing but fuel and grub bills to pay.

Richard's boat was originally built in Vancouver by a fisherman named Patty Flynn, who decided in 1974 to build a larger boat. While on a visit to Vancouver at that time, Richard bought the *Norah Flynn* and had immediately jumped into salmon gillnetting. Over time, he also tried his hand at crabbing and halibut fishing. A year or so on and the Japanese decided to create a new market for British Columbian herring roe. Richard heard about the new fishery while in the Savoy Hotel's bar in Prince Rupert and followed an old-timer's advice: "You boys get over to the fisheries' office; they're selling herring licences for the first time!" For $250, he became one of the first licensed herring fishermen in the Prince Rupert Fishermen's Co-operative.

Richard had chosen to anchor in the Princess Royal Island bay because it was roughly equidistant from Skincuttle Inlet, located in the southern part of the Queen Charlotte Islands [Haida Gwaii], and Nootka Island on the northwest coast of Vancouver Island. Running to either location would take twelve to eighteen hours across very exposed waters. Richard expected that the next herring opening would likely be in one locale or the other and he wanted to keep our options open.

Richard had a generous spirit and a strategic mind, with critical thinking skills sharply honed during his student years as a junior chess champion in Ontario. He also had balls of steel backed up by incredible determination, all the right ingredients to survive and thrive on the risks and adventure offered by British Columbia's wild West Coast. "Boogie till you puke!" was one of his favourite guiding principles. "Let the good times roll!"

Not everyone in our community did survive. Just three years earlier, five of our friends drowned outside of Holberg Inlet off the northern tip of Vancouver Island when an unpredicted and sudden fall storm, with winds topping eighty-six knots, capsized the two boats that had been travelling together. One of the fishermen who died was Thomas Szczuka, one of the partners in the land co-op that Richard and I had started ten years earlier on one hundred sixty acres on Porcher Island, along with Geoff Potter, Bill Edbrooke and a few other friends. Tom's death cut pretty close to the bone for me: he left behind his wife and four young children.

In truth, I wasn't too enthusiastic about commercial fishing after Tom died. He was the most recent addition to a long list of fishermen and mariners from the Prince Rupert region that I had met and been friends with over the previous sixteen years who had lost their lives to the sea. But I had a wife and two-year-old daughter to care for, really enjoyed spending time with Richard and knew that the money would likely be pretty good, possibly providing sufficient income for a full year in a matter of five or six weeks of work.

We waited at anchor for the announcement of the next opening for a couple of weeks. The smaller aluminum herring skiff (colourfully named the *Silver Bitch*) that we fished from, hand-pulling the herring nets over a bar to land the fish, was tied up alongside the *Norah Flynn*, with some old car tires hanging in between the two boats to keep them from bumping together. When running around the coast, we would tow the *Silver Bitch* about thirty metres behind the *Norah Flynn*, with a rubber tire halfway down the tow line to absorb shocks between the waves and sometimes a tire thrown off its stern to make sure it towed in a straight line.

As it happened, shortly after the weather forecast, the DFO announced over their radio channel that the next opening would begin in forty-eight hours at Nootka Island. Late in the afternoon, just as it was turning dark, we fired up the engine, turned on the radar, pulled the anchor and motored out of the inlet into Hecate Strait. With both of us wearing sound protection headsets, we could faintly hear The Eagles's "Hotel California" playing from the car cassette player mounted on the ceiling of the wheelhouse, which we turned up to full volume. The song was competing with the high-pitched, deafening throb of the boat's 6-71 GM diesel engine that Richard and I had repowered the *Norah Flynn* with a few years before. As forecast by the Canadian Coast Guard radio, outside the protection of the anchorage there was a modest, steady wind from the northwest. We set a southward course for just west of Cape Scott on the northern tip of Vancouver Island, with the plan to skirt the cape in the passage between it and Triangle Island, about nine nautical miles seaward of Cape Scott. From there, we would run down Vancouver Island's west coast, past the entrance to Winter Harbour, where Tom and the others had drowned, past Solander Island off the Brooks Peninsula [Mququwin]—a notoriously windy and dangerous spot that stuck out from Vancouver Island's west coast like a hitchhiker's thumb—and from there to Nootka Island, where Captain Cook made the first European landfall on Canada's Pacific coast in 1778.

The going was great for the first six hours or so, but the northwest wind seemed to be picking up. By that time, we were approaching Cape Scott and could see the lighthouse's slowly flashing white light a couple of kilometres to our port side.

Soon, there was no question the wind was picking up. With a following sea and increasingly larger waves, the *Norah Flynn* would swerve at the top of a wave passing beneath and sort of slide down the back side. We had decided not to throw a tire off the stern of the *Silver Bitch*, the idea being that it would just slow us down and was not necessary in the light seas that we expected. As the wind rapidly increased over the next half hour, the *Silver Bitch*, which was really just a flat-bottomed aluminum barge, was being blown toward the stern of the *Norah Flynn*. We started worrying that it might be blown against the stern of the boat, or even crash on top of the stern deck. This was becoming more than we had bargained for. Ordinarily, when making long runs like this, Richard and I would take turns on the wheel for a couple of hours each, either napping or making meals on our time off. Well, there was no sleeping now, or eating. The rough motions of the water and wind were beginning to knock things around the cabin and the bow of the boat was coming perilously close to diving underwater as it was pushed by the stern wind, sliding down each wave.

Around 2 a.m., a couple of kilometres down the west coast of Vancouver Island, we decided to reverse direction to the northwest so that we would at least be facing the wind, have more control over how the *Norah Flynn* handled the oncoming waves and have the wind keep the *Silver Bitch* behind us instead of possibly running us down.

The strength of the wind kept building. We had undoubtedly made the right decision in reversing direction to face the wind but it sure didn't solve all our problems. We were now steering out toward open ocean against very steep waves. The boat would crest a wave and crash down the other side. Soon, the *Norah Flynn* began digging into the oncoming waves, with a rush of whitewater flooding over the foredeck and washing up against the windows of the wheelhouse. It felt like being in a shoebox that was being shaken nonstop with great ferocity. In sixteen years of fishing, I had been out in severe weather plenty of times, but this was crazy. The *Norah Flynn* was a good sea boat but I was afraid it might have met its match. I considered trying to call my brother, David, who was two years older than me and still living in Manhattan where we had grown up, to say goodbye, but it was too noisy and rough in the wheelhouse to do much else than hang on and try to keep my balance.

Meanwhile, the tow line to the *Silver Bitch*, notwithstanding the shock-absorbing tire in the middle of the line, would slack off for a moment with each wave and then snap taut with enormous power. Over the noise of the engine, the wind whistling through the mast's rigging and the crashing waves, we shouted to each other, debating whether to cut the *Silver Bitch* loose, but that would mean losing our fishing season. We then discussed the possibility of one of us trying to jump into the *Silver Bitch* to throw a tire off the stern, but ultimately decided that would be far too dangerous. I tied a rope around myself and secured the other end to the mast and, while Richard steadied the boat against the oncoming waves, managed to pull an additional extra-long and heavy tow rope out of the storage area below the stern deck. Waves and spray were washing over the deck. Together, between waves, Richard and I managed to loosen the tow rope to the *Silver Bitch* and extend it by about sixty metres.

However, by then the boom on the mast had broken free and the mast itself was showing an uncomfortable movement with each lurch of the boat. Worse, the oily water in the bilge was higher than it should have been and was sloshing around. It looked like one of the two bilge pumps had stopped working. By this time, it was around 6 a.m., still dark, and we had jogged about seventeen nautical miles out to sea. We decided to call the Canadian Coast Guard. About an hour later, a military plane came by and circled a few times overhead. They advised that they could send a boat out if necessary. We agreed to stay in contact.

By early afternoon, the wind had died down a bit and we decided to change course again and head for shelter on the east coast of Vancouver Island. Just as we started in toward Goletas Channel, the Canadian Coast Guard rescue boat showed up and offered an escort. With daylight fading, we followed the lights of their boat into their rescue station in Bull Harbour on Hope Island. Stepping off the boat and onto their moorage dock was a fine feeling. We spent a couple of hours straightening out the boat, securing the mast and fixing the bilge pump, and then we spent the night there. After thanking them in the early morning, we took off again for Nootka Island. The wind had died down and the run down the west coast to Nootka Island was smooth as butter.

Years later, Richard wrote some reflections on his years of herring fishing:

> I may have bullshitted a couple of things long ago, but nowadays, when I look back, there's a lot of blurring and dissociation between events and time—especially with herring fishing, where I remember scenes clearly. I remember: setting a net just off a rocky shoreline in spawn water; corking two nets outside of me at night; the net tangling in the projecting branches of a fallen, sunken spruce and turning an abrupt ninety degrees as I made the set; anchoring the net; and then loading up the 3.6-tonne skiff in no time, while keeping the net from getting fouled in every direction. And it's at night: incredible stars, al-

> most windless and hardly anyone else out shaking while we're LOADING UP! Yet I'm not sure exactly which year or season it was, or who I had as a deckhand.
>
> You need reference points, like the anchors at each end of a net, to establish the frame for the canvas you're going to paint on, even in a freestyle impressionist manner.

We ended up doing very well financially that herring season of 1987. Richard began making plans to rebuild the wheelhouse on the *Norah Flynn*, which was damaged after the thrashing from the storm. I, however, decided to look for another way to make a living. I thought to myself, *No point getting older if you don't get smarter!* With two dozen friends lost to the sea, I figured it would be purely a matter of time before my own ticket came up.

A couple of weeks after the herring season was over, Lorrie and I travelled to Vancouver with our young daughter to visit friends and relatives. The weather there was fantastic, warm enough to be outside in a T-shirt in April. Rain-laden Prince Rupert was lucky to get one day like that in a year. Seduced by the good weather, we decided to move to Van-

Herring fishing was lucrative, but it was risky business.

couver. Two months later, we were on the ferry south from Prince Rupert and arrived in Vancouver on June 21, the summer solstice.

We immediately started looking for an affordable place to rent. The third place we looked at was a basement suite on East Seventeenth Avenue, a block off Main Street, and was much nicer than the other two. Several adjacent, well-kept houses on that street were all painted the same colour and were owned by the same landlord, whose first name was Thomas. He was a soft-spoken gentleman in his late fifties or early sixties and had an Irish accent. After we signed the lease agreement, Thomas asked us what we had been doing prior to coming to Vancouver. I said that I had been commercial fishing around Prince Rupert.

"Oh!" he said. "Which boat?"

"A few different boats," I replied, "but mostly the *Norah Flynn*, a thirty-six-foot gillnetter."

Thomas's eyes twinkled. "Well, how about that! My brother, Patty Flynn, built that boat and named it after our sister, Norah."

Oona R

Norman Cheadle

Prince Rupert was the end of the line, the terminus of a long trek north from Guatemala along the spine of the North American Cordillera, the hitchhiker bearing instinctively seaward. Leaving behind the dry Mesoamerican landscape, I regained the USA and slalomed across the "asphalt seas of the great wasted land," another feckless avatar of Odysseus, but a lot less cocky than the hero of *Been Down So Long It Looks Like Up to Me*. Back in Canada, I found myself thousands of kilometres distant from my original point of departure, a small Ontario town on Georgian Bay, my pokey little Ithaca. Nineteen years old, a skinny, road-toughened rat, I marvelled at the not-yet-wasted lands of British Columbia. Somewhere around Quesnel, the cliché "God's country," heard for the first time, rang like a bell summoning the alienated to the way and the life. *Yes!* answered my thirsty soul. My body, emaciated by deserts and dysentery, was avidly drinking in the forest green, thrilling to the Skeena's final descent into the sea. It was the month of May. The ascetic season was over. The great northwest was beckoning.

My first memory of Rupert is waking up early in a pup tent in a park overlooking a harbour alive with brightly coloured fishboats scurrying in all directions. My desire was instant and uncontainable: I wanted to get aboard one of those! My pockets were empty, I needed a job and there before me lay the perfect solution. No more desultory thumb paddling, hooking rides in tin-can vehicles slithering over blacktop. No more ironic, faux epics: it was time for real boats, real work and the adventure of authentic life. Something in the land and seascape of the North Coast made you believe everything was possible, right here, right now, all around you.

The pup tent belonged to an American I'd met on the road somewhere in Northern California, an ex-junkie recently out of jail and headed for Alaska in search of a new life. We had little in common other than our existential destitution, philosophically assumed. He talked about Billie Holliday and Aldous Huxley's *Doors of Perception*. I enthused about Jack Kerouac, the Beat poets, the City Lights Bookstore reverently visited a few days earlier in San Francisco. Together, we tramped the wharves from Cow Bay to Fairview looking for a chance on a boat. When a gruff old Scotsman said he could take one of us, not both, my erstwhile road companion, glancing over at the ferry dock, quickly ceded the place. He would be on the next sailing for Alaska.

The crusty old mariner guffawed when I said I'd sailed small craft on the Great Lakes. I was as green as they come, my ignorance of sea, coast and fishboats absolute. If the conditions of my hiring were explained to me, I didn't hear or understand them. And I didn't care. I had nothing to lose and this was the chance of a lifetime, a portal to something grand. Few details of our departure remain in my memory; so new was everything, I was like a child learning to compose a picture of the world. He gave me a pair of gumboots and fitted me out with "oilskins," as the old man called the Helly Hanson raingear that was charged against my account, which later took a big bite out of my first meagre settlement at the Prince Rupert Fishermen's Co-operative.

The *Oona R*—the toponym an obscure rune to me—was a typical West Coast–style, fifty- or sixty-foot wooden longliner. The octogenarian skipper, Red, who had once clubbed seal pups on the ice floes off Labrador, was taciturn and tough as nails. Cooky, a bent, toothless Icelander well into his nineties, could still coil a skate of gear in a pinch but he seldom left the galley, except to shuffle out on deck to fetch a red snapper for a chowder or a chicken halibut for supper. Crude, unsanitary cuisine for sure: in the bait shack, we sarcastically dubbed him Snow White, but I've never forgotten how delicious that fish tasted, day after day. As inbreaker, I was under the tutelage of a pair of twenty-somethings from Terrace. One was a tall, sinewy white guy, whose name I can't recall and who seemed to know his way around. His more knowledgeable buddy, an Indigenous man, went by the name of Mick. He was the unofficial deck boss.

Mick emanated a quiet authority. His demeanour was calm, his voice soft, his economy of movement elegant and apparently effortless. A couple of weeks into the trip, he lapsed into a deeper quiet, no longer kibbitzing with his white sidekick. To Cooky's dismay, he almost stopped eating and only nibbled at lightly buttered soda crackers. That he managed to continue working with the same undiminished vigour still amazes me. Later, in town between trips, I ran into him at the bar. He was riding a powerful flood tide of alcohol, but his immaculate self-control was intact, its surface just faintly rippled by unseen tide rips. To everyone's dismay, he didn't show up for the second trip. Recalling Mick now, after many decades, I still wonder what was going on beneath that surface.

As soon as the *Oona R* left Rupert harbour, I was immediately, totally lost. The first few days were a blind, heaving, turgid snarl of hooks, lines, chopped bait, anchors, scotchmen, flagpoles, fish guts, wind and rain.

Gradually, I began to find my way and I was fortunate in that I suffered no abuse from my deck-mates, unlike other inbreakers. When we hauled the gear, Red came on deck to man the roller, manoeuvring the boat with hydraulically connected remote controls. If a really big halibut came up, he'd ask for help to gaff it aboard, using the roll of the boat for leverage. One day, a two-hundred-pounder required the extreme measure of enlisting the greenhorn's help. My gaff joined two others already embedded in the massive flounder's head and I heaved for all I was worth. Up over the rail came the fish, the arc of its momentum and the boat's roll knocking me ass backwards into a sloshing pen of not-yet-dressed fish, the monster's tail thwacking me as I squirmed free, quick as an eel and as slimy too.

The general hilarity touched even dour old Red. "We'll make a fisherman of you yet!" he cackled, gleeful but not unkind. Only now do I realize he was likely expressing acceptance. After that first three-week trip, I made a second.

Everyone who has spent time at sea holds memories of ineffable joy, despair and beauty. The moments of sudden insight or revelation are even harder to put into words. It was an afternoon in mid-July, the weather calm. The skipper had decided we needed to take on fresh water. Leaving the gear to soak, we ran from wherever we were, maybe Milbanke Sound, into Klemtu. It was a novel break from routine and it felt like a holiday. From Finlayson Channel, we slipped in behind Cone Island to tie up at the Klemtu dock. I was minding the hose as it filled the freshwater tank, idly staring at the forested slope of the island cone that plunged into smooth, dark water. In contrast to the relentless commotion at sea, all was utterly still. Suddenly, my perception changed and the surroundings took on an intense immediacy: the tree-clad mountain, the island, the whole vast land in the embrace of seawater. It was as if the world had become present in its full-bodied reality, a vibrant three-dimensionality that was somehow new. As though a two-dimensional veil had fallen away, the shroud of signs, words, images, concepts, ideas and all the maps and charts we humans use to navigate existence. A moment of communion with the Real, above or beyond or beneath language.

The following summer, 1974, I deckhanded on the *West Point*, a salmon troller. For three wonderful months, the skipper-owner Gord and I plied the waters north and west of Haida Gwaii. We often fished at Rose Spit, a place that inspired mixed feelings already suggested by the taut violence contained in its name, the mystic rose impaled on a sharp stick. People used to say the west coast of the Charlottes was the end of the world. While there is inhabited land to the east, north and south, it's true that to the west lies only the immense Pacific Ocean. And yet the pointed, northeast corner of Graham Island felt more "end of the world" to me than its west coast, where cozy beaches are festooned with bamboo and glass balls, friendly messages from afar.

The Hecate Strait was liable to be treacherous. Wind and tide could suddenly whip up waves like teeth snapping above hidden turbulence that could foul a troller's lines, especially at the spit. There, Hecate, haunting the crossroads between worlds, harries Dixon Entrance in a fraught, watery confluence that ceaselessly grinds the edge of Rose Spit and hones its lethal vanishing point. No surprise, it could be a fishy place. We worked the spit a lot, a tad obsessively. Often, we were the only boat. At the end of a day's fishing there, we'd run to Tow Hill [Taaw Tldáaw] and drop the hook. We were far from shore but it was comforting to have that solitary nub in sight, its thumbnail cliff poking up from the flatland beach, a peg around which to cast a long, imaginary beach line lest we slip off the edge of the world during the night.

A calm evening, a ruddy twilight deepening: it was time to pick up the gear, leave the spit and head for Tow Hill. As usual, I was alone in the stern cockpit, spooling in the last stainless steel line. It was behaving strangely, weighed down almost vertically. *We've snagged something*, I thought. *Maybe a waterlogged timber*. But as the thing ascended, the deadhead began to grow features and a grotesque face emerged with a thick-lipped, obscenely wide mouth. Surprise speared my guts, shock opened a gap, terror came spilling in. Slowly, laboriously, the line came up, the hydraulics straining. Just as the monster's face neared the surface, the mouth yawned open, gaping like a sea anchor. An enormous ling cod, with great reluctance, let go of the firmly hooked young coho it had swallowed, leaving it partially digested but still quivering and dangling from the line. Languidly, in dreamlike *ralenti*, the big fish let itself fall away and melt into the dark.

The mystery now solved, panic gave way to awe. Ling cod, salmon and human-in-boat were all seamlessly connected by a single, unbroken line. Dressing salmon, I'd already witnessed how live needlefish can sometimes wiggle out of their predator's sliced-open stomach. Suddenly, the primordial mosh pit, its indiscriminate life-and-death exchange, had extrapolated its reach infinitely. No hard border separated higher lifeforms from lower, complex from primitive, above from below; I, too, was one more small fish wriggling in the shape-shifting continuum. This awareness wasn't thought. It resonated bodily, from sternum to skull, a wave pattern in a hollow chamber. As at Klemtu, my mind played catch-up after the initial synoptic perception: the boundless process of life's metamorphoses included the hominid latecomer with its improvised strategies for survival, clever but hit and miss, the troll lines of our puny epistemologies scratching the surface of the vastness.

Much later, Bill Reid's magnificent sculpture *The Raven and the First Men* brought back that experience to me in a different light: the beginning of the human lifeform, our emergence from the marine underworld. Sure, it was a pretty neat trick that, thanks to Raven, we got to clamber out of the clamshell onto the beach at Rose Spit. But Ling Cod, whether Hecate's familiar or Raven in disguise, reminds us where we come from and where we always return because we never totally leave.

Sometime in the early eighties, the *West Point* was found adrift in Dixon Entrance. Gord by then was working his boat alone. He was a decent guy who, as they say, had issues: he drank too much. I wondered if it was near Rose Spit where Gord tumbled off the stern and into the night.

In 1973 or maybe 1974, I met Paul. In the beer parlour at the old Prince Rupert Hotel, his wiry figure was clenched over a copy of the *Prince Rupert Daily News*, his dark eyes probing, ruthlessly interrogating its flimsy pages as though alchemically trying to will a bit of gold from the dross. We immediately became friends. In our many conversations, an overarching theme was "petrochemical civilization," its unsustainability and what to do in the face of so much calamity. He introduced me to Funktion Junction (as I mentally spelled it) and the alternative community nestled in little enclaves around Rupert harbour and beyond.

Norman fished on the *Cape Devon* in the early 1980s.

The two satoris at Klemtu and Rose Spit came to be reference points tethering my life's drift to the North Coast, like the psychic Tow Hills. Paul became a third peg, human and social, our friendship reinforcing the clothesline mooring that kept me coming back. And so, in January 1978, Helen and I moved from Toronto, where we had been based, and settled in Prince Rupert. As Helen recounts in her story "Turned Inside Out" in *Gumboot Girls*, it was thanks to Paul that we built a cabin at Crippen Cove, using materials salvaged from the waterfront building that housed Funktion Junction, slated for demolition in February. We thus joined a heterogeneous bunch of strongly self-reliant individuals bound loosely together by a co-operative sociability, as richly documented in the anthology *Gumboot Girls*. All of us shunned consumerism and the kind of meaningless work later described so trenchantly by anthropologist David Graeber in his book *Bullshit Jobs*. Instead, we pursued that "passion for the Real," which, according to philosopher Alain Badiou, drove all the radical movements of the twentieth century. We beachcombed, built boats and houses, fished, gardened, taught school, planted trees and homesteaded on remote islands. We practised the art of Haywire daily, repairing, inventing and improvising with what was at hand. Salvaging at the Prince Rupert dump was as much an exercise of creative fun as of ecological conscience. Not Freud's reality principle: the Real was the ground for our play.

In September 1983, a fishing accident ended my time on the northwest coast. A helicopter plucked me off the deck of the *Cape Devon* and dropped me in the hospital in Queen Charlotte City [Daajing Giids]. Not long after, back in Rupert, I bought a beater, packed it in and moved down to Vancouver. There was no going back.

Still, all these decades later, fishboats often shape my dreams, in moods ranging from euphoric to oppressive. On my watch, the wheelhouse morphs into the cockpit of a seaplane flying high and free; then, it's a Boeing 747 and I have no idea how to land. Or we are travelling through channels deep in the Central Area, the waterways growing ever narrower and shallower, until suddenly, absurdly, the boat is locked high and dry in an asphalt parking lot with no exit.

Wide awake under the summer sun, however, my little sailing dinghy traces tentative arcs on Lake Huron's North Channel. Small islands sing on the northwest horizon. My sails greedily gulping the fresh breeze, bow slicing through blue water, the hull hums and my body remembers.

Warm thanks to Helen Heffernan for valuable feedback on the first draft of this piece.

Pansy May

Dave Prosser

My appreciation of boats began in 1959. At the age of nine, I moved with my family from Banff to the Saanich Peninsula. We were befriended by an older guy who owned a small, rocky nugget of an island off Canoe Cove. On an early visit, he took me to a small cove, put a life jacket on me and set me free in an eight-foot pram dinghy. I still remember the overwhelming sense of freedom pulling out of the cove and watching my concerned parents getting smaller and smaller.

Boats of one form or another were an important part of my formative years: log rafts in irrigation ponds, steel pontoons in small creeks, salvaged, leaky seine skiffs, a beautiful twelve-foot clinker rowboat, an eight-foot El Toro sailing dinghy. I quit university in 1971, having decided that I didn't really want to become a teacher, and bought a pretty ex-gillnetter built in Sointula in 1929. I spent a couple of years living aboard and cruising the inside of Vancouver Island.

In 1977, after having spent a year and a half exploring Southeast Asia, my money exhausted, I wondered what came next. I got a letter in Bangkok from my best friend who told me he was marrying a Haida girl in Skidegate. That solved that dilemma. Her parents ran the Sea Gay Hotel in Masset and after the wedding they offered me a job as Mr. Fixit in the hotel for six dollars an hour and a free room. I spent the winter there patching drywall and gluing urinals back together.

Eventually, having missed out on a boat I tried to buy and tiring of the Sea Gay circus, I went to work with John Vogelaar rebuilding the *Finella*, an old, forty-five-foot seine boat that had sunk in Masset Inlet. I fished halibut with him in 1978. It was an interesting summer learning about rebuilding and rigging an old boat, the art of longlining and the realities of the fishing industry.

Delkatla Slough in Masset was a busy, vibrant place: crab boats, seine boats, trollers, gillnetters and halibut boats. Several young guys had bought boats and joined the established fleet, which consisted of numerous Haida, pioneering families and a smattering of refugees from the Canadian military base in Masset.

In the fall, I heard about a boatyard in Dodge Cove, across the harbour from Prince Rupert, that had a contract to build four fifty-foot wooden trollers. The fishing industry was thriving. The roe herring fishing had

The year 1979 was a bumper for fish, with salmon gorging on the herring and needlefish at the Dixon Entrance.

experienced several years of almost unprecedented wealth. Much of this money was being funnelled into the building of new boats. I heard that the legendary Iver Wahl and his sons were leading the crew in their old shed in Dodge Cove. The timing was good. I was footloose and single, and several years working as a carpenter had fed my fantasy of becoming a boatbuilder.

Sometime that fall, I learned of a troller in Masset that was being put up for bids. It had belonged to Paul White, a Haida man who had died. It was yet another pretty thirty-seven-foot, double-ended troller, called *Pansy May* after his daughter, built in the village by Joe Edgars, one of the many noted Haida boatbuilders. It was essentially a one-man spring salmon troller, with a high bow, a beautiful sheer line, a fine, narrow beam and a double-ended stern. My friend Sparkle commented one day, "You know, from a distance and in the dark it's really a pretty boat." I had $4,500 from my halibut crew share from the previous season and naive ambition. I had never trolled before.

Against all odds (and with the help of a sympathetic banker in Masset, a government-sponsored Fisheries Improvement Loan and the support of Al Shepherd at BC Packers in Prince Rupert), I managed a successful bid of $55,000, of which $52,000 was the current value of the A licence. Once the stars in my eyes had set, I realized that although the machinery and bottom of the boat were good, the topsides were essentially rotten.

It was a huge decision. Having spent most of my twenties as a semi-hippy (I always worked and I always washed), the thought of the debt scared the shit out of me! I endlessly consulted the *I Ching* for guidance until it eventually told me, "Stop bothering me, do what you need to do." Wilfred Bennet, my friend and a noted Haida shipwright who was pivotal in rebuilding the *Finella*, also finally got tired of my endless quest for guidance and said, "For God's sake, if you want to do it, do it."

I sat on the shore of Masset Inlet one day in a state of deep indecision. I watched another troller catching the tide past Entry Point and heading out to sea. Watching them go as I sat on the beach, boatless, tipped the scale. I signed the papers and committed myself to $50,000 debt for a rotten boat and a fantasy. I moved into the very funky fo'c'sle and started work. It was April 1979 and the season had already started. The main deck was rotten, with the mast sagging in the fish hold. I jacked up the deck beam under the hold, bolted in a length of angle iron, ripped out the rotten deck beams and laminated construction-grade 2x6s into beams supported by joist hangers as a temporary fix. I smeared the cedar deck with Gluvit to slow down the leaks, cut new cedar trolling poles and generally tried to make the boat seaworthy.

One day, a young woman named Maureen came down the dock. She was an apprentice carpenter from Whitehorse and she wanted to go fishing and was ready and willing to go to work on *Pansy May*. I told her I couldn't pay her for her help until we went fishing. She moved aboard and went to work.

On July 1, we were finally ready to go. We spent the night in 7 Mile Point [Mia Kun], a small harbour eleven kilometres, or seven miles, out of Masset, on the edge of the fishing grounds. I had still never trolled. The next morning, an older fisherman agreed to take me out on his boat to show me how to set the gear. We returned to 7 Mile and then Maureen and I untied and pointed the boat west. There was a stiff, northwest breeze blowing and it was a beautiful, sunny day. We got all six lines out and we were fishing!

After a short time of revelling, it was time to check the gear. We both climbed into the cockpit and engaged the gurdies. Immediately, a hydraulic hose on the back of the wheelhouse ruptured, spraying hot hydraulic oil over the boat, decks and us. I bolted through the spray to shut off the hydraulics. I had bought a large selection of trolling gear from a retiring fisherman and had spread it out on the hatch. The gear was drenched in oil, I was drenched in oil, Maureen was drenched in oil. She was also seasick and decided to retire to the bunk.

Just then, my friend and former skipper John Vogelaar, who was running from Prince Rupert to fish halibut on the west side, called me over the VHF radio. He was bringing me a small skiff I had left in Rupert. I explained my situation. He pulled in close and launched my skiff. When I pulled it alongside, I found in it nineteen litres of hydraulic oil and a six pack of beer. It soon became clear that the hydraulic hoses were rotten beyond repair. With Maureen in the bunk, the bow still pointed west into a steep, westerly chop, I climbed into the cockpit and proceeded to drink all six beers. Then, I roused Maureen from the fo'c'sle and began the tedious process of retrieving the gear.

My first impulse was to simply cut the lines at the davits and call it a day. But the thought of replacing all six lines of gear, trolling wire to cannon balls, was too much. Instead, I put on a pair of gloves and began hand-over-hand hauling the 1/16-inch trolling wire aboard while Maureen spun the gurdy spools by hand. I don't remember how long it took but it was very slow and painful. We turned *Pansy May*'s pretty stern to the wind and returned to Masset. Thus ended the first day of my new career. Once in town, Maureen decided that she didn't want to go fishing that much, packed her gear and bid me a fond farewell. Then began the job of scrubbing the boat, replacing all the hydraulic lines and painstakingly scrubbing the oil off all the fishing gear.

Through my contacts on the dock, I met Stibby, a Haida man who had trolling experience, and we once more went to sea. The rest of the season went relatively smoothly: there were many glitches but none proved insurmountable. The year 1979 was a bumper for fish, with Dixon Entrance alive with herring and needlefish and the spring and coho salmon that were gorging on them, and the prices were good. *Pansy May* kept running and Stibby and I established a working relationship. By the middle of September, despite my being a greenhorn and having a haywire boat, I had made $55,000. I can't imagine what the highliners made that summer.

Well, I said smugly to myself, *there's fuck all to this!*

I quickly tired of the congestion and mindless merry-go-round at the top end of Coho Point, which had been named the Circle Jerk. I decided I couldn't afford a better boat, so I began to rebuild *Pansy May*, weed out the haywire and get her in shape to venture around Cape Knox and explore the west coast. I leased a stall in a boatshed in Dodge Cove and began the painful process, living aboard while I ripped and tore and rebuilt. The first winter, I tackled the main deck and put in an insulated, fibreglass fish hold.

Dave purchased *Pansy May* from the late Paul White, who had named the vessel after his daughter.

The next summer, a troller called the *Sunland* snagged one of its stabilizers while entering 7 Mile in a westerly blow and was wrecked on the beach. That fall, Wilfred strongly suggested that I salvage the wheelhouse as it would nicely replace the phone booth–sized wheelhouse on *Pansy May*. The salvage was an adventure that warrants another story. I sent it to Rupert and spent another winter in the boatshed. Fast forward to next spring: a little late and tired, I left Rupert and headed west.

It was a beautiful, calm, sunny afternoon when I dropped the gear at Shag Rock and pointed the bow toward Langara Island, where my girlfriend, Karen, was working. These were the days before the blight of the sporty lodges and Henslung Cove was an all-weather haven for the troll fleet with a small restaurant, a gear store and bootlegged beer.

It felt so good to be fishing with a new wheelhouse, a fibreglass trunk cabin and foredeck, and a dry bunk. I caught a small spring salmon that lay in the checkers. It seemed auspicious to eat the first fish of the season. I walked to the stern, stepping on the bulwarks. I let go of the davits and reached for the short rope that was always hanging from the boom. I used this pig tail to pull myself out of the cockpit and it was one of those subconscious actions, as the rope was always there. However, while hurriedly re-rigging the boat after a winter in the shed, the rope had slid ahead on the boom. It wasn't there. I stood momentarily without either hand holding on. I teetered briefly and then I fell backwards off the stern of the boat. My first reaction was to turn and swim for the stern but there was nothing to grab. At its two-knot trolling speed, *Pansy May* started sailing away.

My first thought was, *I'm in really deep shit*. I was four nautical miles off the beach, *Pansy May* was on autopilot, I had no deckhand and there were no other boats around. My second thought was, *The pigs*. I kicked straight out from the boat and luckily intercepted the port pig, a slab of Styrofoam clipped onto the trolling wire that was trailing off the end of the trolling pole, following the stern lines behind the boat. At least I was still attached to the boat. My next move was to kick off my brand new, expensive Schneider's gumboots. So, now what? It was a long way to Langara. There was only one way back to the boat: up the wire, a twisted, 1/16-inch stainless wire with small brass marks every two-and-a-half fathoms to keep the troll gear spaced.

Each thought process was very simple and very clear. I suppose that it is part of the survival instinct. It was clear what the consequences were: if the wire slipped in my grip, it would cut into my fingers with disastrous results. I was aware that I had to grab the wire and give it a partial twist so it wouldn't slip and then pull slowly and steadily. Fortunately, my winter of work had left my hands calloused. Slowly, hand over hand, I pulled myself toward the boat.

As I got closer, the tagline pulled vertically down from the end of the trolling pole. As *Pansy May* was a small boat and the gear didn't have a large spread, this put me only several metres outside the stabilizer line, which was positioned partway down the pole. I was able to kick over and grab on. Fortunately, I had half-inch poly lines from the stabilizer lines to the boat so I could retrieve them when it was time to raise the poles. The next step was to transfer to these lines and pull myself to the side of the boat. *Pansy May*'s dramatic sheer lines resulted in relatively low freeboard midship. I was able to swing a leg up, wedge behind the aft stays and roll over the rail and onto the deck. Woohoo! I was aboard!

I quickly stripped off all my clothes and went to sit in the wheelhouse. I started to shake. I suppose it was shock setting in. Although I knew it wasn't a good idea to drink when in shock, I poured a large glass of Scotch. I didn't care about future medical repercussions. I was alive. After finishing the Scotch, I went out and hauled the gear. It seemed like a good excuse to quit early that day.

On reflection, it was interesting how pivotal the seventies were to this story. As a young man, I experienced a huge amount of freedom in lifestyle and choice and I had amazing opportunities. A certain naïveté allowed me to take advantage of relatively easy financing and opportunity in the very last days of a thriving fishing industry. At the time, people asked me, "What are you doing? It's over."

Indeed, in the eighties, things changed dramatically. Interest rates skyrocketed, my loan peaking at 23.75 percent. Fish stocks depleted and prices plummeted because of the new fish-farming industry. But the seventies had laid the foundation: the commercial fishing industry was not dead; it was evolving and it remained a viable and rewarding choice. I persevered. With my great partner and a strong, young daughter, I forged a life and lifestyle beyond my early dreams. As Wilfred said, "If you really want to do it, just do it."

Ranger and *Nowthen*

Alan Carl

I grew up in Victoria, BC. When I was seven years old, my father launched a boat he had built in the backyard. It was a powered, thirty-one-foot houseboat with a scow hull, built with plywood and construction lumber and appropriately named the *Carlsark*. Our family spent many weekends and summer holidays cruising mostly around the Gulf Islands.

In 1972, at the age of twenty-one, I found myself in possession of a retired gillnetter named the *Ranger*. It was thirty-one feet, with red cedar planks on oak frames, and it was fairly beamy with a bulging transom stern. The hull looked faintly east coast but had been built locally. I had purchased it almost sight unseen at an auction of fishboats that the Department of Fisheries and Oceans had bought to reduce the number of boats in the salmon fleet.

Wooden boats moored in the Fraser River tend not to leak very much. Cotton caulking may be prone to rot but river silt can fill the gaps. The *Ranger* must have spent considerable time moored in the river. After my first voyage to Sidney on Vancouver Island had washed out the silt, the boat started to leak. I had it hauled out and hired a shipwright to do some caulking and from him I learned the rudiments of the skill. The *Ranger* continued to leak, especially in rough weather, but not nearly as badly.

The next year, I came back to the Fraser River and began living on the boat. Tied up at the government dock in Steveston, the *Ranger*'s seams gradually filled with silt again. In the spring and summer of 1973, I helped my high school friend John Secord build a new fibreglass gillnetter with help from various contractors, including a Japanese shipwright. By early August, we were on our way north to Prince Rupert to catch the tail end of the salmon gillnet season. I made one gillnet trip with him before flying back south.

Back in Steveston, I made friends with a couple renting a small house on a large lot planted with old fruit trees. I fixed up a small, abandoned outbuilding nestled under a large apple tree, installed a wood stove and moved in, living a rural lifestyle half a block from the main street. I had the *Ranger* hauled out and put on blocks in the Kishi brothers' boatyard nearby. The Kishi brothers looked after the gillnet fleet of the BC Packers Imperial Cannery.

In the early spring, I fished with John in earnest. We fished the whole coast, first gillnetting roe herring and then longlining halibut in early May.

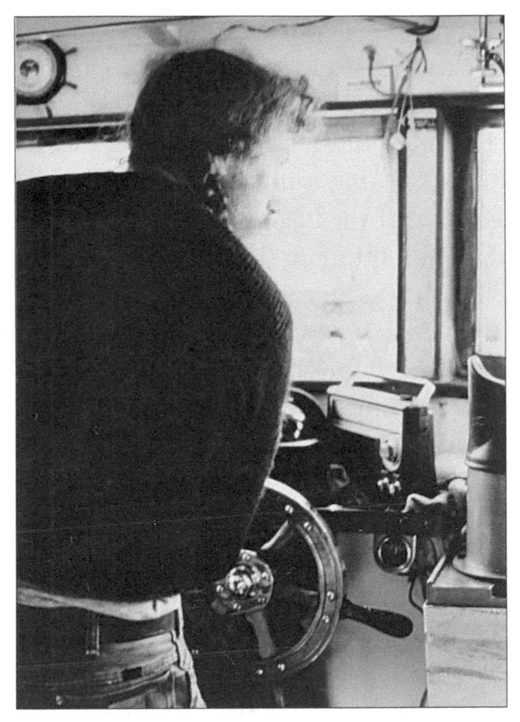

Alan's nautical experience began early—many weekends and summer holidays were spent cruising the Gulf Islands with his family.

Returning to Steveston in July, I continued the rebuilding of the *Ranger*. With my limited woodworking skills, I usually ended up tearing out days' or weeks' worth of work and redoing it, but I did learn. I replaced the transom stern (twice) and raised and extended the main deck over where the gillnet drum used to be. The *Ranger* was built without a keelson, with the ribs stretching full length from one side to the other, a quick and cheap construction method. The Kishi boys suggested this was the cause of the chronic leak and advised, correctly, adding some floors or partial bulkheads to stiffen things up. After taking their advice, the leaking stopped.

By August 1976, I was ready to travel up the coast in the *Ranger*. For navigating, I had a compass and a large-scale chart. For emergencies, I had an old ship-to-shore AM radio. Fran and Steve Morrow from Humpback Bay, Porcher Island, accompanied me. I had decided to live year-round on the North Coast, close to the fishing grounds. I had made friends with numerous young people living on Digby and Porcher islands as well as in Salt Lakes and Prince Rupert, and I decided to explore a bit before settling in one spot.

I found a deckhand for the Hecate Strait crossing wandering the docks in Prince Rupert. He was a lad of maybe seventeen years wanting to return home to Skidegate. We spent two days anchored in Larsen Harbour at the north end of Banks Island waiting for an early September gale to go by, then set out in calm weather. The calm did not last long. By the time we were two-thirds of the way across the strait, it was blowing a stiff southwest breeze, about twenty-five knots. Due to the shape of its hull and having no rigging or stabilizers, the *Ranger* became alarmingly active. Then, I noticed that the engine was overheating. Discovering that there was no water in the cooling system, I tasked the deckhand with fetching buckets of seawater to keep topping up the expansion tank. He hauled seawater until we eventually made it to the dock in Queen Charlotte City [Daajing Giids]. Without helping to tie up the boat or saying goodbye, he was up the ramp and gone. The next morning, I discovered that the sloshing of the bilge water under the engine had dislodged a hose from the thru-hull fitting to the cooling pipes, spewing the engine coolant into the bilge. It was an easy fix.

After a few days in Queen Charlotte City, I set out solo to explore the South Moresby area. With ten days of ideal, clear, calm weather, I had an idyllic time, anchoring in a different spot each night, and with good jigging. As it was late in the season, the whole area seemed deserted.

One night, I stayed in Bag Harbour at the south end of Burnaby Strait. Early next morning, stepping out on deck, I slipped on the first frost of the season and fell overboard. The *Ranger* had flush decks and I hadn't gotten around to installing bulwarks. Luckily, there was a tire hanging over the side that enabled me to scramble back on board. Being naked, I didn't even get my clothes wet. I had no need for coffee that morning.

My friend Pierre, whom I had met in Steveston, was working a handlogging claim near the north end of Burnaby Strait with a fellow named Paul. I stopped for a visit and was offered a job for a couple of weeks setting chokers. As Pierre had lost a leg in a logging accident, he had had trouble operating in thick bush. We didn't always adhere strictly to the handlogging rules, especially on misty days when the forestry plane was unlikely to be flying. I continued sleeping on the *Ranger*, which was tied along with Pierre's tug on the outside of log booms sheltered behind a point. One morning, at about two, I awoke to a raging gale. It was the first of the autumn storms known locally as Pebble Rattlers. The boom had broken free from the shore, swung around and was drifting up Burnaby Strait. The *Ranger*, now on the exposed side, was being pounded against the boom stick it was tied to. Luckily, the engine started right away and, without getting dressed, I managed to cut the tie-up lines and power away. Nudging the beach behind the point, I tossed out the anchor with a lot of line. It didn't drag. In the daylight, we discovered that the boom had miraculously held together and fetched up on a nearby island. Pierre's tug, being steel, was unharmed. The *Ranger* had a stoved-in plank above the water line but was otherwise fine.

After my short career as a handlogger, I spent a couple of weeks hanging around Cumshewa Inlet before returning to Queen Charlotte City for the winter. By March, I was ready to return to the Prince Rupert

Nowthen, a thirty-six-foot salmon troller, was built in 1954 and turned out to be an excellent sea boat.

area, as I needed to be there by early April to prepare for the halibut fishing season. I also knew that my chances for romance were much better there because of the influx of women working in the fish plants for roe herring season. Geoff Potter, whom I had met a few years before in Crippen Cove, foolishly agreed to accompany me. We waited a week for a good weather report before deciding to go anyway. We left on a calm, crystal-clear evening, planning on a daylight landfall on the mainland side. A breeze soon came up and, by the time we could see Bonilla Island lighthouse, a full southeast gale was blowing. We were being tossed about like a cork but everything held together, except the galley. The counter and cupboards I had made from an old, wooden fish crate chose this moment to break loose, threatening to pin us against the other wall. Geoff managed to wrestle it back into position and drive in a few spikes to fasten it to the floor. Once we finally made it to Freeman Pass, we anchored to have a meal and a good sleep.

Soon after arriving in Prince Rupert, I moved into a moldering old cottage in Dodge Cove. Later that spring, on returning from a halibut fishing trip, I found that the owner had returned. He had recently been released from a mental institution. I moved back onto the boat.

Then I met Dolly. She was also interested in rural island life. We spent a week on the *Ranger* visiting Richard Fish in Serpentine Inlet, twenty-six nautical miles south of Prince Rupert on Porcher Island. Dolly was considering joining the group that had purchased one hundred sixty acres of land there but decided against it. Later that spring, she moved into a room in a communal building known locally as Function Junction and I joined her. The building, the former workshop and offices of the Armour Salvage Company, which operated tug and barge services for years in Prince Rupert, was large, wooden and built on pilings over the water, just north of the train station. It was a great place to enjoy the summer. I built bulwarks for the *Ranger* and installed a mast and poles with stabilizers, making the boat safer and more seaworthy.

That September, Dolly and I moved into a small house that became available in Crippen Cove. It was an uninsulated shack with no electricity or running water but it was home. The *Ranger* was moored in Prince Rupert or nearby Dodge Cove, as the tidal flats by Crippen made it a poor place to keep a boat with a keel. By then, I was searching for a fishing vessel of my own.

I found a thirty-six-foot salmon troller in Victoria, smaller than I wanted, but I was concerned about going too far into debt. The *Nowthen* was built in 1954, had a deep wooden hull and was powered by a Volvo Penta diesel engine. I chose well, as the *Nowthen* eventually proved to be an excellent sea boat for its size.

Heading north with the new boat in December, Dolly and I decided to visit friends who were stationed at Boat Bluff Lighthouse near Klemtu. We anchored in calm weather and went ashore to enjoy a good stay and dinner. It was dark when we emerged to find no sign of the *Nowthen*. I was not looking forward to the phone call to the insurance company explaining how I had lost the boat within a week of purchasing it. Our friends got on the radio asking passing boats to look out for the missing craft. Luckily, a mariner spotted an anchor light close to the rocks about half a nautical mile north. Launching a skiff, we found that the *Nowthen* had re-anchored itself about thirty metres from shore.

I spent a few weeks in Prince Rupert Harbour gearing up for the roe herring gillnet season, then Dolly, Steve Morrow and I were off, back down the coast for the first opening at Denman Island near Comox. As the season progressed, we fished our way back up to the North Coast. The year 1979 was a bonanza for roe herring fishers. Japanese buyers were on the grounds with suitcases stuffed full of thousand-dollar bills, bidding up prices to unheard of levels. I had only two seasons of experience as a deckhand in the fishery. Our catches were not large but the big prices made it worthwhile.

Next came salmon trolling. I had a lot to learn in the new-to-me

Fishing was a family business for Alan—by the time his sons were ten or eleven, they were crewing on fishing trips.

fishery. By the end of May, Dolly and I were trying for spring salmon on the north coast of the Queen Charlottes [Haida Gwaii]. We had lots of snarls and not very many fish. After a couple of trips, we decided that Dolly should stay home. She was having a difficult time, being pregnant with our first child. Thanks to a good salmon year with decent prices, my modest catches made for a reasonable season.

Our son, Leon, was born in November. That winter, I removed the rigging from the *Nowthen* and beached it in a stall in Melba Anderson's shed in Dodge Cove. In the main part of the shed, Rick Sobel was constructing the hull of the *Rupert Pelican*. We had plenty of visitors and lots of laughs. I tore out the main deck, sistered the ribs in the fish hold and added an extra fuel tank behind the hold. I raised the main deck, replacing it and the bulwarks in wood. I put in some long days as the deadline to leave for herring fishing approached. I had help with the final caulking in the evenings from a couple of guys who were working for Alex Spiller in the former Wahl boatshed. I kept my fingers crossed, hoping the fresh cement wouldn't wash out of the seams when we encountered bad weather in Milbanke Sound.

Herring season was a washout because of a union strike. I didn't belong to the union but there was nowhere to deliver my catch. My application to join the Prince Rupert Fishermen's Co-operative had not yet gone through. A slow salmon season and rising interest rates made the winter of 1980–81 rather lean. We did have lots of firewood and good crabbing at our doorstep.

In February 1982, I partnered with Richard Fish for the herring season using the *Nowthen* as the mother ship. We fished Denman Island and then headed north. Concerned about missing the Queen Charlotte Islands opening, we picked the worst time in weeks to cross Hecate Strait. Halfway across, in the dark, the towed herring skiff began surfing the swells, threatening to smash into the stern of the *Nowthen*. We did not have enough tires dragging behind the skiff to slow it down. We lengthened the tow line and carried on. Soon, the skiff flipped when it hit a trough and the tow line snapped. In the dark, with a huge sea running, we didn't try to pick up the tow line again because of the risk of fouling the propeller with the floating polypropylene line. Near dawn, we made it to anchor in Jedway Bay. The opening was a few days away, giving us time to borrow a skiff and fish the rest of the season. In May, I received word that my skiff had been spotted floating upside down in Alaskan waters near Cape Muzon. The US Coast Guard had pumped it out and towed it to Ketchikan. Dolly and I, with two-year-old Leon, made the trip to tow it home.

In October, our second son, Shawn, was born. By the time the boys were ten or eleven years old, they were crewing with me fishing salmon and halibut. I did not encourage them to make a career of fishing. I considered it to be a sunset industry. In the years since, I have continued my love affair with old wooden boats. At one point in the late 1990s, I owned three, with a combined age of one hundred sixty years. I found I couldn't keep up with the maintenance and still make a living. I am presently, in 2023, down to one, the *Karmsund*, a forty-four-foot longliner built in 1944.

Sailfish and *Crocodile Rock*

Douglas Laird

In 1972, I stayed in Prince Rupert for a week before boarding the *Northland Prince* ferry to Masset. I had arrived in my friend's green MG Midget convertible from Cree Territory in Northern Alberta to harvest magic mushrooms. I stayed behind while he went over by seaplane. It rained like I had never seen it before, dropping twenty-five centimetres in twenty-four hours. After a week of meeting the most interesting people lodging at the Native Friendship Centre, I watched the *Northland Prince* crew load a car by lifting it into the hold with the deck crane. The crew cast off the lines and the vessel steamed out past the Prince Rupert Fishermen's Co-operative, where I had lunched a few days earlier. A fresh seafood cafe was located right in the fish plant at that time, where I met a few friendly fishers who amazed me with stories of the scope and number of species sought out by the industry. It was a bonus to meet a Métis friend there, a fisher from Northern Alberta who had moved to BC to join the salmon gillnet fleet. I remembered being thrilled to learn that they fished prawns in Canada. More than a decade later, I would see the bounty myself while prawn fishing in Work Channel, where one hundred fifty traps yielded five to ten eighty-litre buckets every day.

Douglas arrived in Prince Rupert in '72 and was thrilled to learn that they fished prawns in Canada.

On board the *Northland Prince*, I met a couple who were returning to Masset with some psilocybin bundled inside paper that captured the spores. The intent was to spread the paper over the swamps where they were picked on the Islands to increase biodiversity and productivity. They kindly shared the mushrooms with me. There were not enough for me to lose the sense of sequential time but I did feel a bit awkward when one of the waiters, decked out with a white coat and a white towel over his arm, slid the chair under me as I was seated. The choice of two meals was included in the fare, which I remember was $15.50. I also remember peering out the door past the tiny bridge deck at the approaching wall of lights on the Masset pier. (Decades later, that pier would become very familiar when I worked as a deckhand on the *Arrow Post*. We made many difficult landings there in the fast-running tides and wind.)

After disembarking, we took the short walk up to a pub that had an amanita mushroom on the door. Ringing the doorbell was the only way to access entry. My stay in Masset lasted just one day as the mushroom fields were flooded by the rain. We flew back to Prince Rupert on a Grumman G-12 Goose, an amphibious airplane that used the fuselage as a hull to land on the water, before climbing up the ramp to dry land. Incidentally, I still use magic mushrooms to this day, as micro-dosing has a profound medicinal effect on anxiety, without the trip. The Haida also knew about the cancer-curing effects of western yew bark, too, another medicine known well locally before modern science.

It was over five years later, in 1977, while sitting in a music venue in Kitsilano, Vancouver, that two women approached me and accused me of a theft at the house where I was living. One of the gals was my roommate; the other was Zoe Roberts, who interrogated me over the details of the accusation. After much assertive bantering, she concluded that I was not the thief, adding that I should join their table for a beer. Years later, I learned it was just a set-up, a ploy to interview me as a deckhand for her fifty-foot sailboat licensed to fish abalone.

One of the people at the table was Zeke, a fisherman who would lease a salmon gillnetter from the monolith fishing organization BC Packers every summer. They were the octopus of the industry with arms everywhere, providing everything you needed from the cradle to the grave. Zeke, like Zoe, was a great storyteller, spinning on about the time when he had stopped over in False Creek with the boat he had leased. He wanted to do some drinking before heading north for the season. Predictably, by the time he left the dock, he was in no condition to navigate. He did get out of the harbour, only to run full speed into the broadside of a freighter. The impact was hard enough to push the anchor winch into the wheelhouse. A nearby sailboat came over to ask if he needed assistance. Zeke replied, "No, eff that, I lost my glasses, I can't see an effing thing."

The reply was to the effect of, "Maybe move your foot? I think you're standing on them," at which time Zeke turned the boat around to run it up on the English Bay Beach. From there, he jumped off the bow and walked over to a phone booth. He called BC Packers to report where they could find their boat and that he would need a better boat. That's the way it was with drinking back then.

Zoe and I spent some time becoming friends over the winter. During those days, she and twenty-five other abalone-licence holders were in negotiations with the Department of Fisheries and Oceans (DFO) to come up with a management plan for the fishery. It was clear to half of the fleet that there were natural limits to the resource but the other half wanted to fish like there was no tomorrow. The management plan was a compromise: there would be a quota after an open fishery and the remaining tonnes would be divided up equally among the fleet. The next summer, the local newspaper featured a front-page photograph of a seiner travelling into the Prince Rupert harbour with a seaplane on its deck. The plane, loaded with abalone, had broken a strut on the floats when it tried to take off. The ensuing radio conversation with the distressed fisher whose catch it was concerned the abalone, not the safety of the pilot or craft. That was part of the greed of some people in those years: they were keen to capitalize on the natural abundance, a bounty that was very obviously in peril from overfishing.

In the spring, I was on my way north on board Zoe's boat, the *Sailfish*, to learn maritime skills: scuba diving, navigation, how to differentiate water tanks from diesel tanks, all from a clever, funny and gregarious looker. The third crew member was Zoe's nephew, Tad Roberts, a talented artist who drew perfect boats with the passion of a naval architect, his trade to this day.

By the time we left Quadra Island, I had heard many stories of adventures on the sea. One fellow had told us how, while repairing his main engine in Campbell River, the boat he had tied to decided to leave in the middle of the night, setting him loose. He had been asleep and woke to find himself adrift in the path of a freighter, which missed him so narrowly that he was swept aside by the bow wave. Years later, there was a similar event in the channel leading into Prince Rupert harbour. The boat *New Start* had veered slightly off course as it was heading out to fish, so the skipper leaned down to correct the autopilot. Before he could finish correcting the course, the boat turned so sharply that it banked sideways right onto its side, with green water rising around the wheelhouse windows! It happened so quickly! A freighter came up behind them and, with its bow wave, lifted the *New Start* onto its bulbous bow. Fortunately, the weight of the water in the crab livewell dragged the boat backward, allowing it to right itself as they began to be pushed out of the way, banging down the side of the freighter. Though dangerously low in the water, the boat did not sink, so the men stood on the stern, where a passing troller picked them up. (The *New Start* had a broken keel and was later loaded onto a barge and taken to Vancouver, where the freighter's insurance company repaired it after a great deal of wrangling in the courts.) The fishermen had quite a story to tell in the Savoy Hotel bar later that evening, laughing through the shock over how they didn't even get their feet wet.

The *Sailfish* was originally built in North Vancouver as a wooden salmon troller to commercial tugboat specs. Zoe acquired the boat and later the licence to fish abalone, setting up a compressor on deck for scuba tanks. I was with Zoe for five or six seasons, two of which we fished Haida Gwaii, as abalone had become hard to find on the mainland. The Hecate Strait provided consistent wind for the crossing and we had some very satisfying sails. However, there is a large shallow area that makes for steep waves in any wind, especially against the huge tides on the North Coast. On one trip, I set up the 111-square-metre genoa and mainsail but as soon as we came out of Cumshewa Inlet, it was apparent by the speed of the clouds that we had to quickly drop the sails. The wind was much stronger than forecast! The waves that smacked the side of the boat were powerful; care was required to not have a hand between the wooden spokes of the wheel, which was spinning hard due to pressure on the rudder. The waves tossed the boat sideways like a toy.

We never actually fished in Cumshewa as we knew there were two boats that had already taken over a million pounds from there, more than the total quota of the entire fleet. The week prior, we fished off the beautiful, haunting beach of the abandoned Haida village Tanu. One day there, during a survey of the bottom in my scuba gear, I came out of a small gully only to be face to face with a beautiful harbour seal resting on the bottom. It gave me a curious look with its big, beautiful eyes and past its enormous whiskers, glanced over its shoulders and back at me, and then pushed itself up and meandered away.

This peaceful encounter was not the case later that week, when I ran into three female sea lions. Their balletic swimming, like a defiance of gravity, was indescribably beautiful to watch. The females didn't have any definite shape to their heads, just faces on the end of long, tapering necks, with extremely long flippers extending midbody. It was all fine and dandy until I looked up and saw a large male coming straight for me. I had to make haste, and after propelling myself firmly with my flippers, I left the water like a whale breaching, so high up I might have fallen over sideways if the Zodiac had been closer. Zoe, of course, was laughing in delight as she knew exactly what was happening and how I would respond. That male lion probably weighed as much as a Volkswagen, an angry VW protecting his harem, guarding their pristine environment against this blue-suited invader.

Douglas joined Zoe Roberts on the *Sailfish*, heading north, to learn maritime skills.

We eventually made it to Prince Rupert, which became my home port for twenty-four years, from 1978 to 2001. For a time, we anchored in a small bay named Isabella Chuck on the northeast side of Porcher Island. We had applied to the provincial government to set up a homestead there only to be refused. One of Zoe's three sons, Richard, a competent fisher and boatbuilder, joined us there with his ex–BC Packers, eighty-foot vessel the *Western Princess*, which was towing his troller, the *Silver Gull*. One night, a group of rowdies chartered Richard's boats for a party. They were rather rambunctious, drinking Richard's homemade beer and potent barley wine and taking magic mushrooms.

I had enough and went to bed, so I missed the mayday that came in as a storm picked up. An American yacht hailed for assistance on channel sixteen. It was anchored a few nautical miles south, between McMicking Island and the eastern coast of Porcher Island. Richard was gung-ho, ready to go, but the pragmatic Zoe suggested he let the Canadian Coast Guard take the lead as a new boat, the *CG 123*, was on its way. However, the coast guard vessel circled in the one- to two-metre waves and ran firmly aground on a reef. So, Richard took off with a crew of drunken sailors. Richard had to ask the *CG 123* to turn off their deck lights, yelling, "I have no radar; I can't see a thing!" They got a line on the sailboat and towed it back to Isabella Chuck while the *CG 123* sat on the reef. Eventually, both boats got all the repairs they needed. (Along the way, Fred Watmough discovered that the twin wheels of the soon-to-be *CCGC Point Henry* were rotating inwards on the top, which created many problems. The boat picked up one-and-a-half knots in speed after the hydraulics were reversed to change the rotation of the propellers.)

In 1979, Zoe gave me the greatest gift of my life. We sailed to San Francisco so that I could participate in a fiftieth anniversary of Ralph Chesse's production of Shakespeare's *Macbeth*. The show used marionettes on four-metre strings and were operated by seven puppeteers and three technicians. I played the Second Witch, who curses Macbeth with a sailor's hex. There is superstition around the curse of Macbeth, but returning to BC in January was a high-risk proposal in any case. We were hit with the tail end of a hurricane for four of the seven days of travel, with eighteen-metre waves that were, at times, breaking over us. The noise was incredibly loud, with powerful frequencies within the range of the human voice. We spent some time without power and steering, but thanks to Zoe's experience, we had lots of sea room for repairs in the westerly winds. It was one of the best experiences a person could ask for and for that I am forever grateful to my skipper Zoe.

The hull of *Crocodile Rock* was designed by Iver Wahl of the well-known boatbuilding Wahl family.

Eventually, I bought a twenty-six-foot wooden sailboat, the *Crocodile Rock*, designed by Iver Wahl, who had designed and built only three sailboats. Shipwright Tom Spiller had the sister hull the *Chanticler*. We did some sailing together and we commercially fished rock cod using rod and reel to jig these exquisite and delicious fish, usually twenty fathoms deep. We would fly our catch to a buyer named Benny in Vancouver. Benny sold our catch in the Chinese fresh-fish market and would take any species of fish we sent.

I got a bow-shaped mast, handmade by a sailor named Malcolm renowned for his mast-making ability, that was complemented by a pretty navy-blue Chinese junk sail from Karl and a bowsprit from a piece of beachcombed yellow cedar that held a western-style jib. A one-cylinder, hand-start Sabb marine diesel pushed it along at six knots. It sailed to the weather helm rather well, likely due to its sizable keel for lateral resistance, a characteristic not known to exemplify the junk-rig experience. The drawback is that I used stays to hold up the mast, which meant I couldn't just let the sail go when the boat got into trouble. When a boat is lying sideways in the water due to a gust of wind, being able to let go the sail is not such a bad feature. Williwaws can provide such breathtaking moments.

SC 109

Ramana Waldhaus

We had three beautiful years in the wilderness, in beautiful and remote Port Louis on the west coast of Haida Gwaii. Roselyn and I had built a little six-sided log cabin beside a creek. It had been our dream to live off grid in an isolated place far away from the madding crowd, from the media, from the many stimuli that civilization offers. We left Queen Charlotte City [Daajing Giids] with our six-week-old baby boy, Telell, to stay in Paul Bower's little cabin while we built our own. Several of our friends let us know that it would be crazy to take a baby out into the wilderness. What if something happened to Telell? What will you do then? No radio, no phone, no roads? We had such faith in the universe, in the kind universe, and believed that our guardian angels would look after us. We knew in our hearts that breastfeeding would keep our baby healthy. It proved to be so. Our experience living there was truly life changing, an experience I cherish to this day.

One of the clear signs that it was time to return to Queen Charlotte City and civilization appeared when we asked Telell, who was then almost four years old, which he would prefer: continue living in Port Louis or head back to Queen Charlotte. The answer was a resounding Queen Charlotte! There were four of us now: Roselyn gave birth to our second son, Taio, in town a couple years earlier. We were a happy lot, grounded and filled with feelings of accomplishment, more in tune. But it was time for a new chapter—Telell had chosen!

As we started loading our boat, the *SC 109*, it became evident that we had more belongings than it could hold. The *SC 109* was a Sunnyside Cannery boat, a small double-ended gillnetter that was long and narrow and probably around twenty-nine feet. Even though we left some things behind, we could see that it was a bit overloaded. I had very little experience with boating so it looked okay to me, just sitting a bit deeper in the water than before. The weather looked perfect, clear and sunny with a gentle northwesterly and a following sea.

That soon changed. About an hour or two south of Port Louis, the weather switched around and a southwesterly began to pick up. I soon realized that we needed to find a harbour. We were just north of Kano Inlet, so we headed for there. All the while, the weather was building. The round-bottomed, shallow-keeled *SC 109* started to roll. I thought

Ramana and his family spent three years living in remote Port Louis, on the west coast of Haida Gwaii.

of putting out the stabilizers but remembered very clearly that a salty, old sailor friend of mine told me to never put out the stabilizers in rough weather and to head to a safe harbour as quickly as possible instead. His reason was that if one of the stabilizers broke off, the boat would most likely capsize under the pull of the other. I started to tack into Kano; the waves were almost broadside. As the waves built and built, the boat started to take on water. There were two storage boxes built against the gunwales on either side of the deck, which were holding the water in because the two scuppers in each were blocked. As the boat rolled, and more and more and more water came in, I started to panic. I froze. All I could do was keep tacking. I knew that we wouldn't make it as things stood. Then I had a vision. I visualized being in the water with Roselyn and holding the two boys. I became very calm and began soothing them and telling them that we would make it to shore. My panic was gone.

Years later, an excellent astrologer was reading my chart and at the end of the session said to me, "I see two past lives of yours. Would you like me to tell you about them?"

"You bet," I said, very curious.

"I see you on the deck of a spice ship sailing East," he said. "It's

Though pictured here in calm water, the *SC 109* weathered a few storms in its time.

nighttime, you have the deck watch, there is a storm and you are washed overboard. There's no way you can be rescued. The ship just sails on. And you know, what's so amazing is that you are so calm in the water." I got goosebumps all over.

"Bail! Bail! Bail!" I screamed at Roselyn. "Take the covers off the lockers and throw the stuff overboard and bail!"

Roselyn immediately went to task. I don't remember where the boys were, but Roselyn had probably put them into the forecastle. I then realized that the load on deck had to go. It all had to go. I remember picking up the two thirty-eight-litre drums of gas and throwing them overboard. Next went our precious cast-iron cook stove. It was small and heavy but I felt no weight. I don't remember what else I threw overboard but eventually the deck was clear. The boat rolled only a little less and the water was still washing the deck, but water was no longer being retained in the two lockers. We eventually made it into calm water. It's difficult to describe the relief we felt. We were now so protected, so safe. From the chart, we saw that Kano was L-shaped and as we motored along the long shaft of the L we could feel the storm and the waves building behind us. It was another relief to enter the protected bottom part of the L shape of Kano and tie up against the log booms that were there.

Throughout the next six days, the weather built up to a righteous storm. Though the seas did not build up where we were tied up, the wind sure did. Periodically, a huge gust would sweep through and lay the boat on its side. But still, we were alive and exhilarated.

When the storm died down, we motored around the corner to check the seas. Before we knew it, we were in rough weather again. I decided to put out the stabilizers as the situation was not as dire as before. We were almost turned when the right stabilizer rope broke. The trusty *SC 109* just did a big roll and righted itself. We felt truly blessed.

SC 134 and *Seabird*

George Farrell

Donnette and I met during our freshmen year at Western Washington University in Bellingham in 1965. She picked me up at a dance in the women's gym and my story is grounded in that relationship. We never missed a campus dance after that. When I became the student manager of the campus cafeteria, I hired Donnette. We both earned seventy-five cents an hour but I got free meals. We married in 1968, becoming the only hippies on campus to be both married and working. Donnette became the house mother to a bunch of ragtag artists, musicians and hippies who named themselves the Dalton Gang and called her Dandy Lion Dalton.

We graduated in 1969, ready to pursue adventure and learning. I had conveniently failed the US military draft but we were both disenchanted with the homeland. So, in 1970, our friend Ian (Greg) Lundquist agreed to drive his van to Prince Rupert where he had relatives so we could visit the remote Queen Charlotte Islands [Haida Gwaii]. Along the way, we slept under the totem poles in Kitwanga. Greg's aunties and grandparents were very hospitable.

From Prince Rupert, we hopped onto a Trans-Provincial Airlines floatplane to Masset. We walked out to the highway from the harbour and stuck out our thumbs. A Volkswagen van taxi stopped and when we said that we were hitchhiking, the driver answered, "I know, but I'm going that way anyway, an empty run back to Charlotte."

He let us off at a hippy commune near Clay Hill, where we spent the night among some colourful people. The next day, we were grateful for a bath and bed in Flo and Louie's Queen Charlotte Hotel and later we met Wow and other characters in the bar. The whole experience was life changing. Donnette and I returned to Bellingham determined to move to this enchanted place to be among special people.

In a farmer's field, we found a 2-tonne, split-axle 1940 GMC flatbed truck for fifty dollars. All it needed was a new battery and some mechanical help from a friend. We named the GMC Perseverance, or Percy for short. Another friend helped us build a beautiful camper while my brother, Dan, built his own camper on a 1950 Ford flatbed. In April 1971, our friends sent us off from Y Road, near Mount Baker, with "Across the Great Divide" by The Band as our soundtrack.

Looking for adventure, George and his partner, Donnette, left Washington in 1970 and headed north.

We travelled slow, especially in the Fraser Canyon. We had large quantities of beans, rice, honey and flour but little money. We took our time enjoying the journey: three weeks to Prince Rupert. Dan had some money and had to lend us the cost of putting our truck on the *Northland Prince* ferry bound for Masset from Prince Rupert. We marvelled at the spectacle of slinging the trucks onto the ship. We ate with the crew, a huge, fantastic meal with dessert, all of which we upchucked in the night as a huge storm engulfed the ship in Hecate Strait. Everyone but iron-stomach Donnette lost the entire meal.

We got off the ship on May 17, 1971, and drove to the Tlell River. We camped at the end of Beitush Road, eating freshly caught cutthroat every morning. Teddy Bellis came along and offered us a job caretaking the Ward and Bellis pig farm, north of Port Clements, for fifty dollars a month and all the eggs we could eat. We spent the summer and fall collecting venison and salmon. Friends from Bellingham came to visit or live and we made many new friends playing music: Dick, Eevan, Ron Souza and Pete the Flute. We also learned all about magic mushrooms.

Teddy noticed we shot hoops and told us that basketball was loved by the Indigenous community locally and along the whole North Coast. So, he got jerseys made that featured long-haired men and the Go-geets became a team. The George Brown Recreation Centre was packed to the rafters at every game throughout the winter and we began a lifelong affair with Haida basketball. We won the 1971 championship but our friends in Skidegate still say we were in it for the showers. Donnette's Crohn's disease caused a major drop in her hemoglobin count and she had to be admitted into the hospital. However, Donnette told the doctors she was responsible for the team's celebration dinner and would have to come back tomorrow. The next day, Donnette and I flew to Vancouver for a blood transfusion. Teddy paid my eighty-dollar plane fare.

We had become great friends with Emil and Elizabeth at their bakery in Port Clements. Donnette took care of their son, Leandre, while they baked and we all played bridge after. Because of Donnette's babysitting experience, neighbours Liz and Archie Stocker asked us to babysit their five children (two in diapers!) for two weeks. Meanwhile, I got a job in the cookhouse at the Juskatla logging camp. This left Donnette with five kids while I went off to work in the crummy early morning every day. Joker Archie called from Germany and told Donnette they wanted to spend another week and got a great laugh out of Donnette's sputtering reaction.

Our friend Bobby got in trouble for growing pot at the pig farm. Now that I had a job, I could bail him out. Four hundred dollars. Bobby paid us back with two lots on Hippy Hill! In the late spring of 1972, we drove the truck to Queen Charlotte City [Daajing Giids], unloaded the camper, truck deck and all, onto our lot.

A few people from Tlell and Hippy Hill got permission to build cabins and have babies at Burnaby Narrows. We helped load them onto Del Fowler's *Bonaventure II*. Donnette and I bought a sixteen-foot Frontiersman canoe and paddled to Burnaby Narrows to visit. Friends drove us to the old logging camp Aero on Gillatt Arm and off we went on a month-long paddle to and from Burnaby Narrows, the adventure of a lifetime. On the way down, we met Karl and Carol doing fish patrol on the *Alp*. It took about a week to reach our friends, then we spent two weeks helping build cabins and exploring the beautiful area in our canoe. On the paddle north, we met Fred and Jeannie Watmough on the *My Jean* just off Windy Bay [Hlk'yah G̱awG̱a], also on fish patrol. We were intrigued by this fish-patrol job and Fred assured us he could help get us a boat even though we had little money left.

George bought the *SC 134* for $600 and a C licence for $10—it was a good start in the quest to fish halibut.

In the early spring of 1973, Fred did indeed introduce us to the manager of the Sunnyside Cannery, who sold us the thirty-foot ex-gill-netter the *SC 134* for six hundred dollars! Chrysler Crown engine and a net drum with an Easthope drive. Our friend Marvin Boyd, who was an excellent mechanic and new seafarer, came over to Rupert to ensure we made it across Hecate Strait. While in Rupert, we bought a C licence for ten dollars so we could fish halibut.

Back at the Charlotte dock, our friend Percy Williams taught us how to tie halibut gear. Joe Tulip, who was in love with barmaid Donnette, took us out to Skidegate Inlet and showed us how to lay and pick up the gear, not that easy off stern rollers. We caught plenty of dogfish. We could only be out for three days, the length of time our ice would last. The first trip down to Laskeek Bay, we never caught a halibut less than thirty kilograms and one was over ninety kilograms. We paid for fuel, the cost of gear and the price of the boat our first trip. We made two more trips without a radio or radar. Our final run back to Skidegate was nerve-racking in the

In Vancouver, George and Donnette found the perfect boat—the *Seabird.*

fog, which spread all the way from Cumshewa Head to the fish plant at Skidegate Landing.

Friends from Bellingham came to visit and we took them to adventure down Moresby Island to Burnaby Narrows. The *SC 134* was crowded with five people aboard. I had no bait, so I used a rag dipped in the bilge to set a trap and filled it with prawns. Our return trip to Skidegate Inlet featured calmer seas and less upchucking.

We applied for the fish-patrol job and got hired. We bought a Mickey Mouse (CB radio) and a radio telephone and left the Charlotte dock for Cumshewa the first week of August 1973. We had a lot to learn that first season and Fred was happy to show us the ropes: lots of creek walking and a bit of observation of the net openings, with morning radio telephone conferences with the office in Charlotte each day. During harbour days, we could listen to reports from patrolmen on the entire coast.

Unfortunately, in the first week of November, just before the end of our contract, our boat sank at the float at the Sewell logging camp during a storm. When the wind switched from southeast to southwest, the log boom broke apart and battered our boat, springing two planks as Donnette, our dog, Pooh, and I jumped to the safety of the float. Again, Fred was his usual helpful self. After three long days, we managed to patch the damage and flush and start the engine. A logger bought the boat for three hundred dollars and moved it ashore with heavy equipment.

I went on a search for another boat early in 1974, armed with the assurance that the credit union would loan us money based on our two lots in Charlotte and a contract with the Department of Fisheries and Oceans (DFO). We searched Prince Rupert and found nothing in our price range, but then I travelled to Vancouver and found the perfect boat. The *Seabird* had done the fish patrol on the coast for the past twelve years. Donnette flew down and, along with our friends Jim and Liz Fulton, who contributed a much-needed skiff, we took two weeks to return to Skidegate Inlet.

In 1974, we salvaged wood from a derelict shack in Skidegate Landing and, with the help of my brother, we built a four-hundred-square-foot cabin with a loft adjacent to our camper. This was our house until 1981, with rainwater and an outhouse. We were the first on Hippy Hill to add electricity. The loft would be a gathering spot to watch the television show *The Waltons* on Sunday nights.

In the fall and winter, we enjoyed basketball, community gatherings and dances, and I played bass in a band. There were dances and basketball games somewhere on island every weekend, a double whammy of fun. Donnette and I became very involved in the Queen Charlotte City Community Club and hosted dances probably once a month. The seventies were a joyous time of island-wide celebration. Although there was violence sometimes, I broke up fights during dances in Skidegate and Charlotte without once receiving a blow. Basketball was for some of us the tie that bound the settler and Haida communities together, although emotions sometimes ran high. Being a basketball referee was also useful in protecting the line during fisheries openings. Going to the All Native Basketball Tournament in Rupert in February was a highlight of the winter. I played with the Percy Williams Orchestra for a dance while all the guys pursued Donnette on the dance floor.

Life in the seventies took on familiar patterns: boat maintenance and fish patrol between July and October and the community club, playing in bands, dances, basketball and work pouring foundations between November and July. Margaret's Café was a favourite hangout.

Fish patrol had its routines. Donnette and I averaged about four and a half hours a day running time observing pink, chum and coho migration between Cumshewa Inlet and Richardson Point in southern Darwin Sound. The other part of a typical day was walking streams, counting salmon and collecting data. We made a report every morning on the radio telephone and listened in to the rest of the patrolmen. Single-sideband VHF radios and radar became required equipment by the late seventies. For most of the decade, the three patrollers on the east coast of Moresby Island would meet in Sewell Inlet for fuel that they could pick up from the

Friendship and mentorship from other mariners was a big part of dock life.

logging camp. Before 1978, we were employees of the DFO; after that, we were hired as contractors.

We were a dedicated bunch and took the job very seriously. I believe it was 1975 when Jack Robinson became skipper of the *Arrow Post*. He was a force, the ultimate seafarer and handyman, a mentor to all of us. I remember that the small, original *Arrow Post* was retired at that time. One evening, as we were anchored in the tiny, sheltered anchorage at Bischof Islands, Jack brought in the new *Arrow* tooting his horn! A difficult feat with a boat that size.

Each patrol would encounter bears on the creeks and close encounters were very common, probably with at least thirty bears a year. We carried various noise makers and used loud voices when communicating. There are numerous funny stories of failed attempts to discourage bear encounters. Bear and bad weather stories filled those years.

In 1977, Jack, Sockeye Sue, others and I started an incubation box on Gore Brook in Charlotte, one year before the official inception of the DFO's Salmonoid Enhancement Program. This experience, and an introduction to the Community Involvement Program, would lead to my full-scale involvement in salmon enhancement and habitat restoration ever since.

I am grateful for a beautiful, supportive and encouraging life partner. The support of so many friends has been amazing. I've been blessed. The seventies in the Charlottes were a truly special time and I owe a lot to some amazing mentors.

Spirit

Lon Sharp

It seems like only yesterday when the tranquil morning air was shattered by a highly animated voice. "Stand up! Sit down! Stand up! Sit down!" it insisted, until I simply had to go out on a limb of my tree house to see what was going on. Below me in the parking lot were a single chair and a lone individual robotically bobbing up and down to his own commands. This would normally seem bizarre if not for the parking lot's proximity to a local Scientology centre known for edgy methodologies.

The coincidence of my tree house locale was due solely to the generosity of long-time school friends renting an old farmhouse at the edge of town in central California. In those days, Peter and Annie were at the heart of many excursions, whether to concerts, theatres, the mountains or into the mind. More than one sunrise was viewed through blurry eyes and a craving for sleep. One time, a group of us took a trip into San Francisco to see the play *Hair*. Since Peter owned a VW bus, he volunteered to be the driver. After a colourful exit from the valley heat, we meandered via the foothills of the Coast Ranges onto the shores of Mark Twain's coldest winter, "one summer in San Francisco." Before us lay the western terminus of the transcontinental Interstate 80. With growing anticipation, we merged our way onto the Bay Bridge, whereupon Peter began to recount the saga of his father's rope company, which had provided the construction safety nets for this very skyway. From exhilarating heights, we pictured flailing bridge workers as they plunged headlong toward the frigid bay, which actually did occur for the sake of a paid day off. Those images stayed with us all the way into the city until we were seated in the theatre. By this time, the illusion of gravity had completely evaporated. *Hair*'s cast members had somehow co-opted Carl Sandburg's "fog on little cat feet" to creep effortlessly over the backs of our seats and onto the stage. All of this took place while the moon was in the seventh house!

After many years in school, I earned a bachelor of arts in animal physiology at the University of California, Davis and the opportunity to simply enjoy the time and place. House painting and groundskeeping were well suited to a bohemian lifestyle of backyard BBQs, local music, cafés, health-food stores and sitting in on chemistry classes. Earlier on I met Maya, who I soon realized was a kindred spirit. She was a sophomore in between sessions and a soon-to-be fellow Argonaut. One time at Guenther's place, we encountered an Alaskan named Jason who was brimming with bush stories and grand plans for an odyssey spanning the coast from Ketchikan to Seattle. I had just been accepted to an out-of-state pharmacology program when Jason called confirming the canoe odyssey. The end of the idyllic Davis days had come.

Maya decided to join the adventure and I turned the tree house over to Guenther, who magnanimously showed his support by driving us Argonauts through the night all the way to Portland, Oregon. From that point, we quickly thumbed a diesel down that took us into the heart of Seattle, blocks from our destination. There, we rendezvoused with Jason and Patti with enough time to prepare before embarking on the *Malaspina* ferry the following day. The *Malaspina* took us up along the West Coast to Ketchikan. For the next thirty hours, we first-time voyagers of the Inside Passage were mesmerized by its stunning beauty. We plopped onto Ketchikan shores 770 nautical miles later and proceeded to the edge of town, where Jason was keeping his magnificent Haida-style dugout canoe. The *Raven Lore* was hewn from a six-metre length of a prime red cedar log and transformed into a sleek, ocean-going craft that handled like a dream. For the next week, our task was to acclimatize our bodies, minds and spirits to this world of ubiquitous water before our canoe trip back down south in the *Raven Lore*.

Lon earned a bachelor of arts in animal physiology at UC Davis before being drawn north on a canoe trip.

While tied up on the docks on our last day in town, we noticed a raucous calamity taking place over on the levee. A flock of ravens was circling above a lone raven caught in a leg-hold trap. Without hesitation, we sprang into action and released the trapped bird. Within moments, the atmosphere transitioned from one of dire frenzy to that of sheer jubilation as all the ravens circled once more and then flew away.

The following day, we officially launched under friendly skies, inflating our lateen sail and spirits alike—until late afternoon, when we were jolted from our daydreams by the ravens who warned us of sail-eating gusts. In that seminal moment, we learned a lesson as we scrambled like mad to get the rigging down. We had the next several days to digest and appreciate the magnitude of Natural Forces before reaching our waypoint crossing to Lax Kw'alaams. This lengthy, non-stop paddle would require an Argonaut demeanour until the *Raven Lore* was safely on the beach. It was indeed a tiring paddle. People came to see the ancient spectre of a cedar Haida canoe and offered us lodging in a small hotel replete with lighting, hot water and a jukebox full of The Beatles' music. At the time, we knew nothing of traditional protocols for visiting canoes and were lucky that our

Spirit was a strip-planked canoe designed in the style of Viking ships.

beachward bow was not mentioned.

Farther south, we were drawn to explore Big Bay's Georgetown Lake, with its defunct, old sawmill perched along the edge of a classic millpond setting. The caretakers shared their space and offered us a tow into town as well as a cabin in Salt Lakes. By now, it was apparent that reaching Seattle was not a reality: Jason was distracted and Patti wanted to go back to Berkeley. Meanwhile, Maya and I thoroughly enjoyed the bustling harbour of Prince Rupert, especially after our previous bush living. The luminescent contrails of darting salmon were everywhere in the evening water, signalling the coming of fall. As a registered university student, Maya needed to reconnect with Davis. After she left, I heard about the Canadian amnesty program that offered no-questions-asked immigrant status to illegal American expats. Although my presence in Canada was purely coincidental, the amnesty provided me with a hassle-free avenue to an extended stay in Canada. No more. No less.

The *Spirit* was equipped with an Ariel-made square sail, allowing the vessel to sail-surf right up onto sandy beaches.

Once I started the North Coast odyssey, I came to realize that some doors are improbable, some doors are unforeseen and others are only open once. Academia could always wait; I had yet to answer those whisperings of the storied Misty Islands.

Many connections were made in the old Rupert hotel, such as my cooking job on the packer boat the *JRD* or the *Silver Triton* ride over to Moresby Camp, where there were seaplanes, seine boats, trollers, leaping salmon and a very small dock overtaken by trekkers, the *Mad Trapper* and a wafting smokehouse. I hired a seaplane to Queen Charlotte City [Daajing Giids]: Margaret's Café, Hippy Hill, Porter's mill, the garbage dump, Sleepy Hollow, the cemetery, Haydn Turner Park and the edge of town. Fall storms were advancing and so was I, from outdoor camping to the old QCC hospital building where I had met Ariel, a new registered nurse. We entered the long winter evening doing night shifts, she at the new hospital and myself in the attic studio carving the Haida village Skedans [K̲'uuna Llnagaay] into cedar boards, encountering spirits and designing a Viking canoe. Long working days brought the completion of the *Spirit*, the seagoing and strip-planked nineteen-foot canoe, replete with a foot-controlled rudder, an Ariel-made square sail, a mast and two sets of oars for stability and propulsion.

Skedans now beckoned from its natural setting near the gateway of Gwaii Haanas. Although much of its beachfront grandeur was ravaged by time, its essence remained. Like a Zen garden, Gwaii Haanas was alive with a transcendental quality that belied the untamed power lurking just below its surface. While visiting, we were surprised by the sudden onslaught of a vicious sou'easter that sent us scrambling for shelter on the leeward beach. There, we hunkered down for a long, unplanned night. For the rest of the afternoon, we sat by the fire sipping hot chocolate, read Baba Ram Dass's *The Only Dance There Is* and witnessed a megalithic Buddha emerge from the nearby rocky cliffs and settle into an unflinching Lotus position as thundering waves crashed onto his lap. With apprehension and relief, we awoke the next morning to find the *Spirit* unscathed.

Like many others, we were drawn to Hotspring Island [G̲andll K'in Gwaay.yaay] for the luxury of heated baths in the wilderness. Unexpectedly, we were also treated to warm hamburgers. *Haw'aa* again, Berta Brown, one of the kindest of souls.

One morning after spending some time in Swan Bay, we headed out into calm water and blue skies. Beyond the mouth, we encountered a growing expanse of whitewater that soon escalated to waves of perilous magnitude. It immediately became imperative to maintain a firm grip on our resolve, our oars and the ocean if we expected to make landfall in Ikeda Cove's opening. Eventually, there it appeared. We paddled into it and another dimension where calmness prevailed. I was thinking that it was good to be alive, to have feet on the ground, to have an amazing fellow Argonaut and to have one more day on this journey. Night was falling, we hadn't yet made camp, a full moon was rising, Hecate was claiming to be smooth and Benjamin Point was waiting. Seduced once again, we realized we were no longer within a moonlit seascape as a black shroud crept out of the west. Instead, we were now in dead-reckoning mode with the merest of distant glints as our guide. Kelp began grabbing at our oars until we eventually felt our way onto a boulder beach to tie up, pitch a tent and then wake up in time to get the canoe back in the water and head for SG̲ang Gwaay. This natural fortress seemed even further enhanced by its isolation and the strong presence of ancient souls. While camping one evening beyond the village edge, we could hear the happy chatter of mothers and children.

Before leaving SG̱ang Gwaay, our most excellent mascot, Puma the black cat, laid claim to his feline prerogative. When we weren't looking, he dragged the remainder of our ling cod meal under a huge driftwood pile and refused to come out. By the time he reappeared, he was near comatose from gluttony. Sorry, Puma!

The skies cleared and there before us lay the southern terminus of our journey: Gilbert Bay, Kunghit Island. In that moment, we became inspired to unfurl Ariel's sail ahead of a gentle westerly that would take us to our destination. As the *Spirit* drew closer, our eyes inhaled the apparition of white-sand beaches garnished with vibrant-green vegetation and basaltic outcroppings. We were so taken by this enveloping panorama that we sail-surfed right onto the beach!

Eventually, it came time for us to make our way back to Skidegate Inlet. We were two different people from the ones who had embarked so long ago.

Sunkid and *Child of the Moon*

For Ken Peerless (1939–2004)

written by Jane Kinegal,
wife for a while, sister-friend always

It must have been quite a sight when Ken Peerless, his pregnant wife, Donna, and their heap of worldly goods arrived on the Charlottes [Haida Gwaii] in the early seventies. The zany cavalcade made its way from Prince George to Masset with, as KP said, "bobtails and tag ends flying." It must have been something to see—from a safe distance. An overstuffed truck and horses were involved, maybe a car and a pickup too. There's a story of their horses escaping after being offloaded from the *Northland Prince* ferry, followed by a chase and recapture. Horsetails flying. I wish now I'd asked more questions.

Ken and Donna have both passed on, but there remains a complicated and affectionate crowd who came together around this much-beloved, sometimes not-so-much-beloved man.

Ken was born in Nelson in 1939. He left to study in Vancouver after high school. His English teacher, Dorothy Livesay, said of the young poets of that place and time that he was the finest. KP didn't breeze this around; another poet of his time told me. Eventually, Ken trashed all his writings, decided to keep talking instead. He could sure tell a story.

Jump from academia to seven years in the Royal Navy: many adventures, many unprintable, I imagine. I'm glad I didn't ask too many questions. Somewhere in there he had a brief career chasing whales, so he knew Rose Harbour long before we bought into the settlers' co-operative. He was a hunting guide near Prince George and managed to put a dying taxi stand back on the road for some lost businessman in Prince George too. Who knows what else he'd been up to before he went west off the mainland to the edge of the world. I do know that sometimes it's good not to ask too many questions.

Ken's gentle and pregnant wife had sensible misgivings about this moving from Prince George to the west coast of the Charlottes, but she was in love and fun loving, too, and eventually agreed to go. Sialun Bay was where they first settled, with the mighty help of friends. Donna had some realistic inklings about how easy it was NOT going to be out there. She flew back to the hospital in Prince George for Tao's birth and, on their

Ken is remembered as a gifted poet—his English teacher, Dorothy Livesay, considered him one of the finest of the young poets.

return to Sialun Bay, the boat that was carrying them sank in the bay in front of their home. Some tins of canned milk brought back for the baby rolled up with the tide after the shipwreck. They had a tiny herd of feisty goats as backup milk supply, too, which was a workable idea until all the goats mysteriously died. Later, a monumental west coast storm ripped the heavy plastic roof off their elegant A-frame, and Ken and his family suddenly became part of history.

For her book *The Queen Charlotte Islands*, volume two, Kathleen Dalzell interviewed Ken. I'm guessing she understood the value of not asking too many questions too. She wrote:

> When asked about the perils of choosing such an inaccessible homesite, young Ken Peerless said, 'Every place demands dues. We find the benefits of what we have out there are well worth the inconveniences.' The birth of their baby son, Tao, in the fall of 1971, kept Mrs. Peerless away only briefly. Her return to Sialun brought home to the couple just how isolated they really were, when the launch taking her back was wrecked in the bay and most of the precious food supplies were lost. Later, Ken had to walk the shoreline to the Naden Harbour logging camp to summon help when the baby's milk supply grew low. A rugged mid-winter hike which took him eight days—and spoke highly of his physical condition from the life at Sialun Bay.[1]

Dalzell didn't mention snow, which Ken told us was "up to my ass" on the journey.

Back in Masset to regroup-restock for another attempt at living on the edge, Ken bought a leaky, old fishboat, aptly named the *Sunkid*. He spent long days making his boat seaworthy. For this next pioneering gig, three households were involved: Ken, Donna and Tao (and Lao, gestating); Paul and Anita Bower; and KP's crony from Prince George Ken Bailey, his young son, Howard, and me, KB's partner at the time. Others came and went when planes flew in or boats passed by. We all moved to the west coast again, to Port Louis, with tag ends flying and supplies to last a good while. I was more attentive to nature than ever before, but there were some maybe natural tensions between the men that I didn't pay enough mind to. We women were quite smug about how well we got on together. Donna and Anita taught me bush cookery and we all figured out how to bake bread in an airtight heater. Donna had booked a floatplane to take her to town to birth her second child. We were afraid dodgy weather would prevent the plane from getting her out in time. KP handed me a Guatemalan midwifery manual, in Spanish, just in case. Studying the diagrams and Donna's belly with full attention, I learned her baby was breech. *Relieved* doesn't half describe how I felt when the yellow tin can showed up to fly her to town.

I was some surprised when Ken Bailey called up the airline to take us out of there one day. He and Howard returned to Prince George and

1. Kathleen E. Dalzell, *The Queen Charlotte Islands: Of Place and Names,* vol. 2 (Madeira Park: Harbour Publishing, 1989).

I landed in Port Clements. Another surprising day months later, Ken, Donna, their children and an assortment of others, fresh from Port Louis, reconnected at the little Richardson house I was looking after in Port Clements. Necessary regrouping began again and again. We were all glad everyone was alive and reasonably well and most of us recognized it's sometimes wise not to ask questions.

I missed a chunk of the Peerless saga when I went to Victoria to work. But when I met Ken again in 1975, he was a born-again bachelor. He'd been given the golden chance to own a new, uptown, fancy-ass fibreglass troller-gillnetter. Logically, he named it the *Child of the Moon*, successor to the *Sunkid*. No more old bilgewater. He suggested I become his partner in life and off we went fishing together.

Ken's new compadres, first in Masset, then particularly Mike McNeill, Arnold Pearson and Herb Hughan in the Queen Charlotte City [Daajing Giids] area, showed him how to become a highliner. With them, we chased salmon and herring all around the islands, sometimes venturing to mainland regions too. I was never employed by Ken. Our new relationship was complicated enough. I grew up near a salmon cannery, knew about fish, was an efficient deckhand, but never his employee. A money

Ken named his new troller-gillnetter *Child of the Moon*, the logical successor to *Sunkid*.

jar that theoretically belonged to us both worked just fine. The people we fished with were true allies, sharing lore and information, inventing codes to send messages on the airwaves, always ready to help. These times together were the finest kind, as KP would say. Mike, Vivian and their lovely daughters, Vicky and Sissy (whose ears sometimes needed to be covered by their cheerful but firm mom); Arnold the gentleman and Nigel, his sunbeam of a son; Cliff Jones, whose wise ways were an example for us all out there; unfailingly good-natured Herb; and Ken, with his hilarious tales and songs: everyone seemed to be their best selves. And herring season was incredible. I reckoned the wildest stories I'd heard about the gold rush were probably true.

I still have some fine memories of my five-plus years aboard the *Child of the Moon*. An iffy memory: a boat race, powered by too much beer. I was furious (maybe I'd not had enough beer) and said I would fish with Kenny again ONLY IF we both had proper and dependable emergency gear. Back in Charlotte, we marched immediately to Meegan's Store and he purchased two bright-orange floater coats that we needed in cold weather (but never again in a race).

A beautiful day: the captain took to his bunk while we were on a long haul back to town after twelve days out. I had clear instructions about the course to steer, the weather was very fine, Hoyt Axton and other tunes were blasting through the headphones. I was content for a good long while. But after too many hours, my thoughts veered toward mutiny. KP always said the *Child of the Moon* was a fishy boat, but that day, it was a definite sea-creature magnet. Just as I was readying to voice my complaints, a line of orcas showed up right beside the boat. I was startled. Maybe they were dolphins? After almost fifty years, the image of the critters has lost clarity in my mind. They began jumping alongside, some on the starboard side, too, racing along and crossing ahead of the bow. My mutinous thoughts and the sea critters were gone in short seconds.

A good surprise: I knew KP had a good understanding of the sea, but my regard for him skyrocketed one stormy day when we were crossing the Hecate Strait to Prince Rupert. We were following the *Haida Warrior*, envying that more seaworthy seiner. The fibreglass *Child of the Moon* was fancy dancing. Swells were smashing over the windows. I understood that turning back had implications and also that it had to be his decision. I respected his sea sense when we turned and scooted back to the dock after bashing about a third of the way across.

My connection with the *Child of the Moon* ended when Kenny decided to deliver some fish caught by another fisherman that by common

KP always considered the *Child of the Moon* to be a magnet for sea creatures, and orca and dolphin sightings were an occasional thrill.

union logic and general common sense should never have been caught or delivered. I never did understand his line of reasoning though he seemed secure in himself that it was the right thing to do. The deckhand involved in this moonlight act was not me, though KP said, "My deckhand did it." I had to tell two of my favourite fleet gossipers, "It ain't me." Word got around briskly. I was off the hook but Kenny's place in the fleet had changed.

KP saw that the fishing industry was changing dramatically. We both began to dream of other possibilities. He assumed he was, like the old song says, here for a good time, not a long time. None of his male ancestors had lived to reach fifty because of a heart issue, so how to realize our "heroic possibilities" was important to both our venturesome hearts. He opted for tropical adventure, I for academia, our child under my arm. He got busy in the Philippines: courting; writing, directing and acting in action movies; writing adventure tales inspired by his new life. He returned to the North Coast each fishing season.

When the *Child of the Moon* unfortunately burned to a frizzle one day, that was it with boats for Ken. He settled in the Philippines with his new cast of characters and sent reams of stories back. He had joined forces with Rose, a young woman with whom he eventually had five bright, lively boys. He returned to Charlotte after a fierce bout of cerebral malaria. Rose and their boys joined him in time and they spent mellow golden years there till two strokes felled him at age sixty-four, way older than he ever expected.

In his "dotage," as he called it, Kenny became political. He was elected as an area director for the Skeena–Queen Charlotte Regional District and he transformed himself into quite the political/technological nerd. Not long before he died, he emailed me this news:

> My website is growing slowly but steadily in readership. Up to 1,500 a week now with a healthy sprinkling of Europeans. When/if it gets to 10,000, I figure to ask for subscriptions of, say, $10 a year—enough money to fly into some of these spots where the US media bullshit is thick and report from on the ground. Yeah. I foresee the possibility of a whole new career of shit disturbing just ahead. CNN should be very afraid. Antonia Zerbisias from the *Toronto Star* has one of those snap-brim fedoras with the press card in the hat band she'll lend me.

KP stories circulated. Our daughter, Quincey, and her husband were in a bar in Washington, DC, chatting with some guy and she mentioned she was from the Charlottes. The guy began telling a KP story. Quincey listened, then explained KP was her dad.

"Be aware," he replied. "The FBI knows you're here if you've ever had email contact with KP!"

Another time, Quincey and I met a stranger on Salt Spring Island. Same thing. He asked where we were from and then launched into a KP tale. He stopped the telling quick when we told him our relationship.

Ken knew how to soar and he wished the same for others. The best, most lasting part of my connection with KP is Quincey, who inherited his best: smarts, charm, generosity, curiosity. She wrote about him after he returned to Canada from his long absence in the Philippines:

> My dad's personality was bigger and more outlandish than I'd remembered. His habit of shouting when he got excited or emphatic alarmed me and he was excited or emphatic about one thing or another much of the time. His views of the world were vastly different from mine and he seemed disappointed that I was content to go to ballet classes and read books; he wondered why I wasn't out having more "adventures." We had the regular teenage-daughter-and-middle-aged-father issues, except with us they appeared reversed. I wanted him to be more responsible, he seemed to think I was a little too sedate.
>
> It wasn't until I quit university on something of a whim to move to a small town in Ireland that we began to see more eye to eye. I'd proven that I had a bit of adventure in me after all and he was proud. I began to loosen up and tried to take my mother's advice to enjoy the good bits of my dad, while ignoring the rest as much as possible.

When Ken lay unconscious, dying in Vancouver General Hospital after his second stroke, the neurologist sat in the corner, clearly fascinated by the parade of people who came to say goodbye. He was waiting for Rose to arrive to get her legal permission to pull the plug on this larger-than-life life, an elemental part of our complex family of DNA-joined and chosen relatives, now including grandchildren as well. I suggested the doctor think "bush," not tidy family tree, and he got it. No questions.

So, Kenny: another Gumboot Guy who showed up on the North Coast in the early seventies. He shook the ground, rippled the water and filled the air with a certain amount of smoke, lots of laughter and many well-embroidered tales.

Tanalorn

For Bruce Anderson (1949–2007)

written by Stewart Brinton

Bruce Anderson was a tall man with large hands, a keen eye and a quick mind. He and his wife had been students at Humboldt State College in Arcata, California. The war in Vietnam sent them north to British Columbia then up to Prince Rupert and finally across the harbour to the boatshed in Dodge Cove, where Bruce began crafting the boat of their dreams. He and his wife were going to traverse the Pacific Ocean, but the dream died with the marriage.

When I met Bruce on the docks at Cow Bay, we had both been traumatized by loss: I was a recently minted widower, he was a recently minted divorcee. We were both displaced Yankees who had been raised in Northern California and were former Eagle Scouts.

I'd been a deckhand on a halibut boat. When the season was over, Bruce suggested we live together in a shack down the path from the boat-

Bruce, with his Nordic features, made an excellent Santa Claus for the kids at Dodge Cove.

shed. There ended up being three of us as I had acquired a girlfriend named Maureen. We were all over six feet tall, squeezed into a narrow room with double-plastic sheeting separating us from the rest of the ramshackle house.

We lit our humble room by kerosene lamps and heated it by stuffing salvaged wood into a compact ship's stove. We passed a long, dark winter listening to CBC radio. Our favorite program was *Doctor Bundolo's Pandemonium Medicine Show*. We also played music together, with me on harmonica and Bruce providing rhythm with a jar of beans. We created an act titled "Duelling Jew's Harps" for the coffeehouse at the Anglican church in Prince Rupert. We played Jew's harps until our gums bled.

Bruce gave me a drawknife and some yellow cedar blanks and taught me how to make oars. I loved making oars because my woodworking skills were minimal and I loved rowing. Bruce had a carvel-planked, double-ended rowboat built in the forties. It was a beautiful boat designed for trolling for spring salmon off Langara Island in Haida Gwaii. In the postwar era, there was a fleet of sprit-rigged rowboats that day fished. The fishermen delivered their catch to a cannery boat in the evening and then pulled their boats onto the beach, with the fishermen living in improvised encampments.

The fishermen that day fished in sprit-rigged rowboats would deliver their catch to a cannery boat in the evening.

The rowboat was sixteen feet in length and had an oak stem, stern, ribs, keel and keelson, with fir planking. It was as stout and steady as a sea duck. It had two oar stations and Maureen and I loved tandem rowing, especially at night with the glimmer of city lights on the water and the rhythmic dip and feathering of the oars, with the click of the oar locks occasionally interrupted by a heron's shriek or the flutter of seabird wings.

One summer, Bruce set up a sprit rig on the rowboat and began sailing in the harbour. I was standing on the co-op dock one day when Bruce sailed in and tied up. A seine boat captain had been watching him through binoculars. He asked if he could have a turn, claiming that he'd been part of the Langara fleet as a teenager. He remembered a friend passing him in full sail while they trolled for spring salmon. His friend was reading a comic book. The captain took Bruce's boat out into the harbour and returned with the biggest smile imaginable. For him, it was Christmas in July.

The rowboat was never given a name and was lost a few years later coming in from Brown's Mill on the Ecstall River. The tow line tying it to the stern of Jimmy Donaldson's tug the *Two Rivers* chafed and the canoe was set adrift in Chatham Sound never to be seen again.

Bruce had strong Nordic features and, with his ruddy cheeks, flourishing beard and hearty *ho, ho, ho*, he made a perfect Santa Claus for the kids at Dodge Cove. He eventually braided his beard. It became his signature look.

In 1978, I was given the chance to become CBC/Radio-Canada's first late-night disc jockey. Two female CBC employees had devised a program to air from midnight to 3:00 a.m. and asked me to be part of their brainstorm. We titled the show *The All Star Herring Revue*. The theme song was Pink Floyd's "Money" from *The Dark Side of the Moon*.

The women on the fish cannery lines had the most gruelling and monotonous chore: standing on a damp cement floor popping roe from pregnant herring hour after hour. My job was to provide music and humour. For music, I had a large record collection and so did CBC. I could play entire sides of albums if I wished. For humour, I created a soap opera titled *As the Brain Drains*. Bernie of the Braided Beard was one of characters, inspired by Bruce.

The show was an immense success. I was told that when the humorous bits in *As the Brain Drains* occurred, the women on the line who had their headphones tuned to CBC Radio would heel over and laugh in unison. The cannery supervisors didn't know what was happening.

The All Star Herring Revue received a fan letter from a long-haul trucker somewhere in Georgia. Apparently, the radio signal bounced against the ionosphere making reception possible in his area of the south. The program lasted over a month and won an award back east for most original programming. The station manager, who had nothing to do with the show, took all the credit.

Malcolm Elder was the caretaker of the boatshed. He lived in a shack beside it. He was in his late sixties or early seventies, physically robust with a shock of white hair. He was a communist/socialist/libertarian who welcomed the influx of educated anti-establishment hippies.

With his gummy smile, Malcolm was always delighted to engage me in tea and conversation. One day as we chatted, he began rubbing grease onto a pair of boots. The grease emitted a pungent odour. I asked him what it was.

"Bear grease" he answered. "It's the best thing for waterproofing leather." That may be true, I observed, but if you were to wear a pair of boots with that goop on it, you'd soon be chased by a pack of dogs.

Malcolm had served in World War II. After the war, he worked in boatsheds. His specialty was using an adze to create a mast from a cant of wood, taking it from four sides to eight and so on until it was fully round, a much-valued skill. He hurt his foot in a logging accident and thereafter walked with a pronounced limp. He eventually got disability, then a pension.

Malcolm lived frugally and over time he saved enough money to build his own live-aboard boat, to be named the *Chilco*. He deeply admired Bruce and often discussed his ideas and plans with him.

Thanks to Malcolm's constant prodding, Bruce finally completed the hull and deck of the *Tanalorn*. The same high tide that launched the *Tanalorn* allowed the keel for the *Chilco* to float in place. There was no champagne or fanfare when the *Tanalorn* was launched, just exasperated relief.

The *Tanalorn* continued to be an albatross around Bruce's neck. It was moved to the dock where it leaked like a sieve. After repairs, it still leaked relentlessly. Years later, the next owner had the *Tanalorn* lifted onto dry land and discovered that the garboard plank had never been caulked and powder worms had eaten tiny, invisible holes into the mahogany planks before they were installed. The subsequent repairs were laborious but successful.

Bruce was also a skilled jeweller. During the day, he was in the boatshed, in the macro world of timber and band saws and planers; then, in the evening he would be hunched over his work table with a coping saw, immersed in the micro world of fine inlay, using mahogany, ebony, ivory and abalone shell.

Bruce was a skilled jeweller, creating unique pieces of abalone, ivory and silver.

Bruce passed away over fifteen years ago and left a legacy of beautiful brooches, pendants and earrings in distinctive designs in silver and gold. He built the *Tanalorn*, his entrance into the fascinating and demanding world of wooden boatbuilding. Subsequently, he worked for a while at Slack Tide Boat Works in Cow Bay. Work wise, that was his happiest time: spending his days in a boatshed, then his evenings fashioning jewellery.

Postscript: I would be remiss not to include the recipe for Bruce's Bountiful Brown Bread. It was a recipe he'd adapted from *The Tassajara Bread Book*. Bruce took joy in giving loaves to people and his recipe passed throughout the Gumboot community, inspiring others to bake his bountiful brown bread. He took meticulous care in his preparations. He used a large porcelain bowl covered with a towel to ensure just the right temperature for the rising and used the driest wood possible to bring the ship's stove to the correct temperature. Once he inserted the loaves into the stove, he would rotate them to allow for even baking.

Bruce's Bountiful Brown Bread (4 loaves)

1. In a large bowl, combine:
    - ½ to ¾ cup molasses
    - 4 cups lukewarm water
    - 2 cups whole wheat flour
    - 2 cups unbleached white flour
    - 1 cup rolled oats
    - 2 tbsp yeast
2. Stir, cover and let rise until doubled. Then, add:
    - 1 tbsp salt
    - 2 tbsp lemon juice
    - 4 tbsp oil
3. Stir well. Add:
    - 1/3 cup each sesame seeds, flax seeds, poppy seeds
    - 1 cup sunflower seeds
4. Stir well. Then, add and stir in, one cup at a time:
    - 2 more cups of unbleached flour
    - 2 more cups of whole wheat flour.
5. Stir until impossible, then knead with more whole wheat flour for 10 minutes.
6. Oil another bowl, put the dough inside and turn it over to oil the top. Cover and let rise until doubled.
7. Remove and divide into 4 lumps. Cover and let rest for 10 minutes.
8. Oil bread pans. Form into loaves, place in pans, turn over to oil the top and cover.
9. Let rise for 1 hour.
10. Bake at 350°C for 50 minutes.
11. Remove from oven and remove loaves from pans onto rack. Brush top crust with oil or butter.
12. Enjoy!

Toker II

Bill Smith

Growing up in North Texas, my exposure to boats and the ocean was limited. Still, because I watched *Adventures in Paradise* on TV, I dreamed of going to sea. Later, as a young adult, I was a deckhand on a merchant ship to Okinawa carrying PX supplies during the Vietnam War. Being on the water and in a typhoon was interesting and exciting, but it lacked the romance of the dream. I wanted to travel among exotic islands and get to know the people who lived on them. That had to wait until I moved to Canada.

In July of 1970, I joined friends who were driving to Prince Rupert from Virginia. They were moving to Canada so their draft-aged son could register with Foreign Board 100, which was more likely than a stateside draft board to recognize his conscientious-objector status as a birthright Quaker. A year later, their goal achieved, my friends moved to New Mexico. Soon after, I left Rupert for California.

Running low on money by the time I reached Vancouver, I decided to stay longer in Canada. I got a job at a lumberyard in Port Moody and rented a cheap apartment in an old hotel nearby. The following summer, I tried fishing in whatever bodies of water I could access from the shore, but I only caught one dogfish off a log boom in Howe Sound and some small catfish in the Fraser River. It was disappointing compared to the large number of edible fish I had caught off the docks in Prince Rupert.

Blaming my poor success in the Lower Mainland on my lack of access to offshore hot spots, I decided to get a boat, something I had wanted since my Texas days. I found an old, inexpensive, ex–Fraser River gillnetter at the docks in Deep Cove. It was a twenty-seven-foot double-ender that was sheathed in thin plywood to strengthen its rotting wooden hull. Rumour had it that the boat, named the *Toker II* by the previous owners, had been used to rob waterfront homes.

The *Toker*'s engine was a twelve-horsepower, two-cylinder Vivian built in Victoria in the forties. It was a bolted-together assembly of large, green-painted pieces of cast iron that looked more like a cartoon than an engine. As with most old, heavy-duty engines, the Vivian was started by hand rolling the flywheel.

Of the Vivian's exposed, potentially hazardous moving parts, the most dangerous was the big, spoked flywheel spinning at the engine's forward end. To enter or leave the fo'c'sle, a person had to pass within inches of it. Being

Bill worked in commercial fishing for forty years, mostly in old wooden boats that required knowledge of weather and maintenance and an abundance of caution.

aware of the risk, I was careful. But not my rescue cat, a little black-and-white male I had found abandoned on the road to Deep Cove. He decided that he needed to jump over the moving flywheel. Fortunately, I noticed him preparing for his maiden attempt and was able to snatch him away. He must have registered my concern. I watched carefully and never saw him try that again.

The *Toker*'s hull leaked at the garboard seams where the plywood skin ended on either side of the keel. I poured Portland cement into the bilge of the boat. The leaking stopped and the extra weight helped dampen the boat's roll. Unfortunately, it also increased the possibility that, if the boat swamped, there wouldn't be enough flotation to keep it from sinking, especially since the deck wasn't self-bailing.

Other changes I made to the *Toker* included the installation of a battery, a wheel-driven automobile generator and an electric bilge pump. I changed the fuel tank, replaced hoses and sealed the rudder tube. Had I known more about mechanics, I would have replaced the self-aligning bearing on the shaft. Installed as a thrust bearing behind a universal joint, it was inappropriate to that application. Remarkably, it lasted a long time before coming apart.

The *Toker* was the beginning of a long, interesting relationship I have had with old wooden boats and old engines. Now, after over fifty years on the water, I realize that some of those boats were not safe. Today, I wouldn't leave the dock in a boat like the *Toker* unless I was bringing along a good skiff.

I practised operating the *Toker* in the relatively calm waters of Indian Arm. Finally, the cat and I headed up the coast. We stopped first at Gibson's Landing and later at Squirrel Cove on Cortes Island. It being the 1970s, the government docks were free, the anchorages weren't crowded and the oysters were delicious. I decided to return to the North Coast, where, although there were no oysters, the fishing was good, work was plentiful and people were easy to meet.

The *Toker* came with a dashboard compass and a small gear anchor but no sounder, radio, radar or even running lights. I added a flashlight, a clock and some tools. Along with a few south-coast charts, I also took a Loran chart (Canadian Hydrographic Service chart 3744) for travelling the waters north of Vancouver Island. It didn't show details that might be useful for avoiding shallow water and anchoring but it was better than a road map.

The first evening, the cat and I tied to a can buoy at God's Pocket, on the north side of Goletas Channel across from Port Hardy. As we were leaving the next morning, a dense fog rolled in. Visibility was about fifteen metres. Straining to see ahead while trying to keep a compass course, we crept between rocks and islands. Eventually, we found ourselves out of the fog and in a huge expanse of water that the chart indicated was Queen Charlotte Strait.

It was blowing a strong westerly. Bucking into increasingly more open, rough water, we were going in the wrong direction, farther out to sea. I was afraid to turn toward the mainland. If I did, during the turn the boat would be sideways to the wind and waves. It might roll too far and swamp.

Anxiety about ending up in Japan finally overcame my fear of sinking. Partway into the turn, a wave caught the side of the boat and laid it over. At that moment, a stay wire attached to the long exhaust pipe let go. When the wire slapped the top of the wheelhouse with a loud bang, I immediately became seasick. (I think the cat had been sick for a while.) As the boat continued turning without swamping and finally righted with its stern to the waves, everything changed. There was no more pounding and no more spray. Steering became easier. Later, I learned that double-enders are good in a following sea. After I found the source of the loud bang and determined there was no damage to the boat, the rest of the crossing was almost fun. It was a little like surfing.

According to the Loran chart, Safety Cove was on the east side of

Calvert Island, in the direction we now were headed. Though the chart didn't show depth or type of bottom, we were worn out and I badly wanted to anchor before dark. Under the circumstances, the name of the cove was enough information for me. When we reached Safety Cove, I went too far in and ran aground in mud and eelgrass. After backing off, I found some boomsticks secured alongside a cliff where there was plenty of water. I put down some tire fenders and tied the boat beside a boomstick for the night.

The next day, travelling in Fitzhugh Sound, north of Calvert Island, I saw a large splash in the distance. Thinking a boat might have exploded, I sped up as much as I could. I watched for smoke, flames or people in the water. When the splash happened again, I was close enough to get a better look. Whales were breaching! I felt like Dorothy. I wasn't in Texas anymore.

The rest of our trip was interesting but relatively uneventful. In Shearwater, I was able to buy some northern charts, which I was using when we finally reached the entrance to Prince Rupert harbour. They would take us past the city to Fern Passage, through Butze Rapids to Morse Basin (chart 3701) and past Denise Inlet to our destination, Kloiya Bay (chart 3703).

It had been a long journey and I was distracted by the anticipation of our arrival. As a result, I didn't notice on the chart the Butze Rapids inset, which warned: "CAUTION: The channel should be navigated at high slack." It didn't really matter: without a tide book, I didn't know what the tide was doing anyway. Thinking back, it was probably near mid-flood when we entered Fern Passage. That was bad timing.

The cat liked to hang out on top of the trunk cabin, away from engine noise and fumes. He strategically positioned himself so he couldn't be grabbed through a wheelhouse window. As we neared Butze Rapids, that's where he was, sitting on the trunk cabin just out of reach.

I looked ahead to the fast-approaching rapids. With the boat in the grip of a powerful current, I could see something was terribly wrong. At the rapids, the water dropped off as if it was going over a low wall. I thought we were about to hit a rocky ledge, where we would hang up and slue sideways; then, we'd roll over and drop upside down onto the boulders below. We might as well be going over Niagara Falls in a rotten barrel half-full of cast iron and cement. I wished the cat was already in Kloiya Bay and I wished I was there with him.

When we hit the drop off, the bow of the boat dove underwater. The cat spread-eagled, with his claws out on the slippery trunk cabin top. To my surprise and relief, he managed to stay on board. When the bow rose and the boat was swept into the rapids, it remained upright and more or less steerable in the swirling water. There was no rock wall with boulders below, just a lot of water being pushed through a narrow opening. After we cleared the rapids, the cat came inside.

When we finally arrived at Kloiya Bay, there was a boat already in the little man-made anchorage beside the campground. The boat belonged to Buster Hill, a retired Prince Rupert fire chief who was working for the Department of Fisheries and Oceans (DFO) as a creek watcher. Back then, people were hired to live near salmon creeks to count fish and prevent poaching during the spawning runs. At Buster's invitation, I tied alongside his boat.

The cat and I lived in a tent for the rest of the summer and into the fall. Buster was staying in a little pan-abode log cabin provided by the DFO. After his contract ended, he invited me to use the cabin. I gladly accepted. With the improved accommodations, we were able to spend the winter in Kloiya Bay.

I could tell by the tracks in the snow that wolves were hunting around the cabin at night. The cat refused to be kept in. He must have had a good escape strategy because they never got him. When the wolves howled nearby, I would open the door and fire a shotgun into the air.

In the spring, I got work at the Prince Rupert Fishermen's Co-operative processing herring roe. I commuted from Kloiya Bay with an old Ford truck I had bought cheaply in Rupert. Often, I had to walk through snow, up to the highway where the truck was parked. During the layoff between the herring and salmon seasons, I met Frank Bennett, who lived on Anian Island across the harbour from the co-op. He invited me to stay there in an unoccupied house. The cat went to live with a nice family in town where he seemed very happy. He was playing with the kids when I last saw him.

Anian had no all-tide dock, so Frank and I put out a mooring for the *Toker*. Eventually, I bought a used, fourteen-foot riveted-aluminum skiff with a twenty-horsepower Mercury outboard. It wasn't a safe all-weather commuter because it was light, but it could be kept in a small, shallow bay near the house, where it was more accessible than the *Toker*.

I lived on Anian for about a year. Around the time I left, I traded the *Toker* for a young risk taker's boat, the *BA*, a double-ended ex-gillnetter built by the Wahls for the British-American Cannery at Port Essington. It was a foot longer and in better condition than the *Toker*, but its motor didn't run. Eventually, I discovered that the end of the distributor shaft was gone, eaten off by salt water. The engine must have been sunk and not flushed afterward. I replaced it with a four-cylinder, F-head Jeep engine that I bought used from North Pacific Cannery. Not long after, I bought the *Cassiar III* from North Pacific. It was a thirty-foot, square-sterned ex-gillnetter powered by a six-cylinder Chrysler Ace. The *BA* and the *Cassiar III* had electric-start engines, which was convenient, but I missed hand rolling a flywheel.

The new owner, with a couple of adventurous friends and a dog, took the *Toker* south. Near Cape Scott, at the northwestern corner of Vancouver Island, they got too close to the beach and ran aground in the surf. A small Primus stove tipped over and, in the resulting fire, the boat was destroyed. The dog and all three guys were okay, but they were on the beach for a few days before a passing seine boat picked them up.

I felt badly about the loss of the classic Vivian engine. Though I cared about the *Toker*, I thought it was lucky that it had burned before anyone died in it. The owner was obviously heading down the long, often-wild west coast of Vancouver Island when the *Toker* went aground. The boat was too old and patched together for a trip like that.

So am I, now. But the places I've been and the people I've met have surpassed my adolescent dreams. I fished commercially for forty years, mostly in old wooden boats that taught me a lot about maintenance, weather and caution. I currently live in a small community on a North Coast island. I'm rebuilding the *Joe's Lunch*, a twenty-foot wooden boat built by Iver Wahl in the sixties as a work boat for the family's commercial boatshed. When finished, I'll have a seaworthy boat to fish from and wander around in.

This place is almost paradise; except I wish there was less rain and more coconut palms.

The *Toker* was lost in a fire, but fortunately no one was injured.

Tomram

Rob Pettigrew

It is 1973. My high school sweetheart, Shirley, had just graduated and, with her newly fledged nursing degree, obtained her first posting at the Queen Charlotte Islands General Hospital. After finishing my summer work, I followed her lead and was hooked from the moment I stepped off the plane in Sandspit. What followed was the best year (well, one of the best years) of my life playing with our friends: "Hey, let's roll another joint" — "Let's go clamming on North Beach!" — "For sure, a big northeast last night, bet the scallops are laying there for the picking" — "Homebrew, anyone?" — "Party at Robert's!" — "The mushrooms are up in Tlell," and on it went. We hiked up Sleeping Beauty Mountain, along East Beach, up to Cape Ball and out to the spit. We did a lot of paddling in our canoe on Yakoun Lake and explored salt waters whenever we could. Every day was magical!

On one of our canoeing excursions, we left Moresby Camp and paddled our way south. As we entered Carmichael Passage, we encountered a beautiful boat, the *Seabird*, coming north, having just come through Louise Narrows. It slowed, then stopped, and two very friendly people standing up on the dodger, George and Donnette, waved us over. From this encounter, we made two lifelong friends and acquired an idea for a new career: fish patrol.

It took a while to get there, but in 1979 I eventually bought a half share of a boat, an ex–Rivtow Straits, forty-seven-foot tug with the enigmatic name of the *Tomram*. The boat was born in 1943 in Bay City, Michigan, and named the *USN 998*. The United States Navy enlisted it to pull targets on the Great Lakes for torpedo practice. It must have had a very long tow line and never towed on a Monday because it did survive and eventually arrived on the West Coast. Although I would like to think that it made its way through the canal and up the coast, I suppose it took a more ignominious route across the Midwest on rails. In 1962, it was registered by the River Towing Company (later named Rivtow Straits) and renamed as the *Red Fir No. 9*. They put it into service on Pitt Lake towing log booms to the mills on the Fraser River. At some point, they moved it north to perform the same service on the Skeena and Nass rivers. Sometime around 1975, the boat was purchased by a private individual and renamed the *Tomram*, a second choice to the reverse of those letters, the *Marmot*, and

Many on the DFO patrol lived aboard their boats and in some cases raised kids on the water.

was used for beachcombing and halibut fishing. Friends bought the boat in 1978 and brought her over to the Charlottes. Jim and Donna Drury bought a half share a year later and we bought the other half shortly after. Jim was a woodcarver by trade and with his skill, expertise and energy we ripped off the old wheelhouse and, in the living room of their hand-hewn cabin, fashioned a new one. Together, we used the boat for handlogging (yarding fallen trees in the ocean for sale) and fishing halibut. We eventually bought our partners out and I began my chartering career.

In those first years, I did whatever charter work came my way: the Geological Survey of Canada, the BC Ministry of Forests, Parks Canada, the Vancouver Aquarium, various private parties and the Department of Fisheries and Oceans' (DFO) salmon patrol. All without really having much experience in anything. It didn't seem to matter in those days: figure it out as you go, with not much in the way of regulations about anything.

In 1980, I began what turned out to be a thirty-seven-year career on contract to the DFO walking creeks, repairing damaged stream habitat and monitoring commercial fisheries in many locations on the east and west coasts of Moresby Island. A book could be written on the history of the DFO fisheries patrol program and all the land-based guardians (dubbed the Freak on Every Creek Program by Jack Robinson, skipper of the fisheries patrol vessel *Arrow Post*) who monitored salmon returns to their respective streams and estuaries. The guardian program fell by the wayside by the early eighties, but the DFO patrol program flourished throughout the eighties and nineties and continues to this day, albeit in a very much reduced form.

There was so much abundance in the seventies and eighties: the salmon, the fishing fleet, the fisher people, fish packers, DFO patrol boats, the charter patrol fleet. All remain but in such a diminished state as to make the seventies and eighties seem like a figment of my imagination. Haida Gwaii had three dedicated DFO patrol boats—the *Arrow Post*, the *Sooke Post* and the *Pillar Rock*—as well as five charter patrol boats, each at sea for eighty-five days from August through early November to monitor the last stages of the returning salmon migration. The charter patrolmen and women lived aboard their boats and in some cases raised their kids on the water.

I continued to work on contract on the east and west coasts of Haida Gwaii throughout the nineties and 2000s, through to the end of the 2016 season. Throughout the eighties and nineties, I only worked in east Skidegate Inlet and west Skidegate Channel; the abundance of returning salmon justified it. Days were full, walking the banks of the streams estimating

Cabin demolition crew Jim Drury and John Weir with the advisory committee, Mike Hennigan and Art Babcock, overseeing.

the salmon populations. If enough salmon were observed in the streams to indicate that the eventual escapement would reach the DFO's target amount (i.e., an estimated ideal amount to produce a good run in the next cycle), the DFO would announce an opening for fishing with set starting and closing times within a day or two. Gillnetters and seiners would run over from all areas of the coast to harvest what was hopefully "surplus to escapement needs" salmon. Openings for commercial harvest were usually twelve hours and would often go on for several days.

The patrolman's day was spent preparing for the fishery, erecting or repairing triangular boundary signs, opening and closing the fishery, monitoring catches and walking streams to determine how close each was to the DFO's target escapement. Eventually, if the target was met, the stream-mouth boundaries were dropped and both gillnet and seine boats could take anything they could catch right to the river mouth. After the fishery closed, our job was to pick up the fish-delivery slips from the packers after the last gillnetter had delivered, often at two in the morning in a storm's driving rain. Catch numbers would be tallied that night so they were ready for a conference the next morning and then it would begin all over again. Often for days.

When I began in 1980, salmon stocks in Haida Gwaii were at peak abundance and supported a vibrant fishery that benefited all the small

Rob bought a half share of the *Tomram*, named for "marmot" spelled backwards.

communities on the North Coast. By my last year, most chum, pink and coho stocks were seriously depleted and have supported little to no commercial fishing effort since. The fishing fleet has been reduced to a small fraction of what it was in 1980 via numerous buyback programs. The three fishery patrol vessels—populated by crews that knew fish, knew fish habitat, knew the fishing fleet and were pretty good at finding the balance of ensuring enough salmon made it upstream to spawn and, if at all possible, provide commercial fishing opportunities that supported local communities—are long gone. The five contract patrol boats on Haida Gwaii, each with eighty-five days of patrol coverage, have been reduced to two boats with thirty-two days on the east side of Moresby Island and twenty-eight days to cover all streams on the west side of Haida Gwaii.

The seventies and eighties were exciting times. The sheer abundance of chum, pink and coho salmon returning to their home streams was, in hindsight, astounding. The reasons for such bounty as well as the reasons why salmon stocks declined in abundance are complicated and due to many combined factors. The DFO believes that ocean survival conditions peaked in the seventies and eighties. Why the decline? Perhaps ocean-survival conditions diminished in part because of climate change? Possible explanations as to why our salmon resource has so significantly declined also include: spawning habitat loss, overfishing, open-net salmon farming in the Atlantic and innovations in technology making fishing efforts so much more efficient.

I pretty much loved every day on the sea with my family, monitoring the salmon runs returning to Haida Gwaii. Although I'm sad to have witnessed the decline of salmon stocks, I have faith that they will one day return in abundance. I could never have imagined such a great adventure when I landed in Sandspit some fifty years ago.

TRN 101

Larry Hill

Larry, his wife, his brother and a couple of friends lived together in a house in Daajing Giids.

I was living in Queen Charlotte City [Daajing Giids] in the early seventies. At Easter time, I had gone up to visit my brother Steve, who was teaching high school in Queen Charlotte City and loved the area. My wife and I decided to return along with our friends Cody and Judy Good. The five of us rented an old house about halfway between Charlotte and the Haida village Skidegate. Our old friend Rags (Ed Regnery) owned the house. He had brought it over from one of the logging camps and pulled it up the beach with oxen. Rags, originally from Holland, was a long-time resident, logger, fisherman, house builder and boatbuilder, one of those amazing old-timers who could do anything. He was always amazed at the books we had and that we would always be looking things up. Rags once said, "You Hill boys probably learned to screw from a book!"

Rags's old house looked over the Skidegate Channel between Graham and Moresby islands. It was a spectacular place to live and a magical time. The air was so pure you could almost bite it. We could watch the fog and clouds come through the narrow opening between the islands and in the distance reclined Sleeping Beauty, a snow-covered, miniature alpine mountain. No television or internet to fill our free time: we all learned to knit, did lots of crafting and played music. Roughly once a month, we would receive a wooden chess box mailed up to us full of Lasqueti Lace, some great homegrown pot from our friends in the south.

One day, Rags came to us with a proposition. A friend of his had left his boat after the season and had decided to sell it, and he thought that we should buy it. He took us over to Sandspit on his gillnetter the *Roller Skate*, one of the boats he had built, to look at it. It was an odd-looking grey boat sort of like a miniature patrol-torpedo boat. It was a thirty-seven-foot-long gillnet/troller combination named the *TRN 101*, with a

In the seventies, there was no trolling season, but gillnetting was more controlled with limited openings along the coast.

seven-tonne A licence, an Isuzu four-cylinder diesel engine and some gear, asking price $7,500. We thought about it for a few days and decided to buy it. Steve and Cody had deckhanded aboard trollers out of Ucluelet but I had only ever sport fished. It was going to be an adventure.

We cleaned up the boat and got some tools through Princess Auto, at that time a mainly mail-order company where you could buy almost anything, including a surplus jet-wing fuel tank if you wanted! The previous owner had fished for Babcock Fisheries, so we established a relationship with them and got some funds to gear ourselves up. The three of us planned on each fishing two weeks on, one week off. We would pool the money, pay expenses and split the profits equally. This worked pretty well. Good trips offset not-so-good trips.

During those times, there was really no trolling season. You could start fishing as early as you wanted or were crazy enough to start. Gillnetting was more controlled with limited openings along the coast. Our first trip was on April 25, 1973, and we headed through the Skidegate Narrows out to the west coast with the net off the drum. It was quite a journey through the narrows, following markers that showed the channel. You had to time the trip at slack tide before the tide changed directions. At full tide, the current could flow up to seven knots, about the speed of our boat. The narrows were well named because they were at some points only eighteen metres wide.

We made our way north to Rennell Sound and fished the Tartu tack along with some other local fishing boats. One of the boats owned by Harold Christianson headed off farther north. Harold fished by himself and would always come back loaded with large spring salmon. Unfortunately, our boat was too slow to keep up with him, so we never found out where he went! These early trips were not that productive but we were learning. It was a wonderful feeling to fill our fuel and water tanks, pack the groceries into every little cubby we had in the galley, ice up and head out self-contained.

We started fishing on the west coast for spring salmon, ling cod and halibut. Then, we would move to the east coast south of Sandspit, Cumshewa Inlet and beyond. One of our favourite spots after a long day trolling was Hotspring Island [G̲andll K'in Gwaay.yaay]. At that time, you could anchor, row ashore, walk through a cathedral-like forest and emerge onto a beach with a small shack and a bathtub sitting on the sand with two pipes flowing into it. You could select the temperature by positioning the pipes, strip off and immerse yourself. Wow. Now, there is a much larger pool with changing rooms. A recent earthquake has affected the flow although it seems to be resuming.

The early summer months brought the coho runs and some of our best fishing where we would catch hundreds in a day. Unfortunately, these coho runs have all but ended. Later in the summer and in early fall, we switched to gillnetting, winding the gillnet onto the drum and heading to an opening. Rags was our mentor here as he had years of experience gillnetting. Rags was an old leftist with lots of stories of the early fishing days and the organizing of the United Fishermen and Allied Workers' Union (UFAWU). He cajoled me into joining and for a time I was the secretary treasurer of the Skidegate Local with Rags as president.

Our first season was limited to the local area and it was during one of these openings that Cody came rushing over to us in a speedboat from Queen Charlotte City shouting that my wife, Robyn, was in labour. He jumped on board and I jumped onto the speedboat and raced back. It turned out we were sitting on a nice set of coho, between sixty and seventy fish. I went immediately to the hospital, where the first nurse that saw me

Opposite: When his wife was in labour, Larry went straight from the boat to the hospital, but a nurse sent him home to shower before he was allowed into the delivery room.

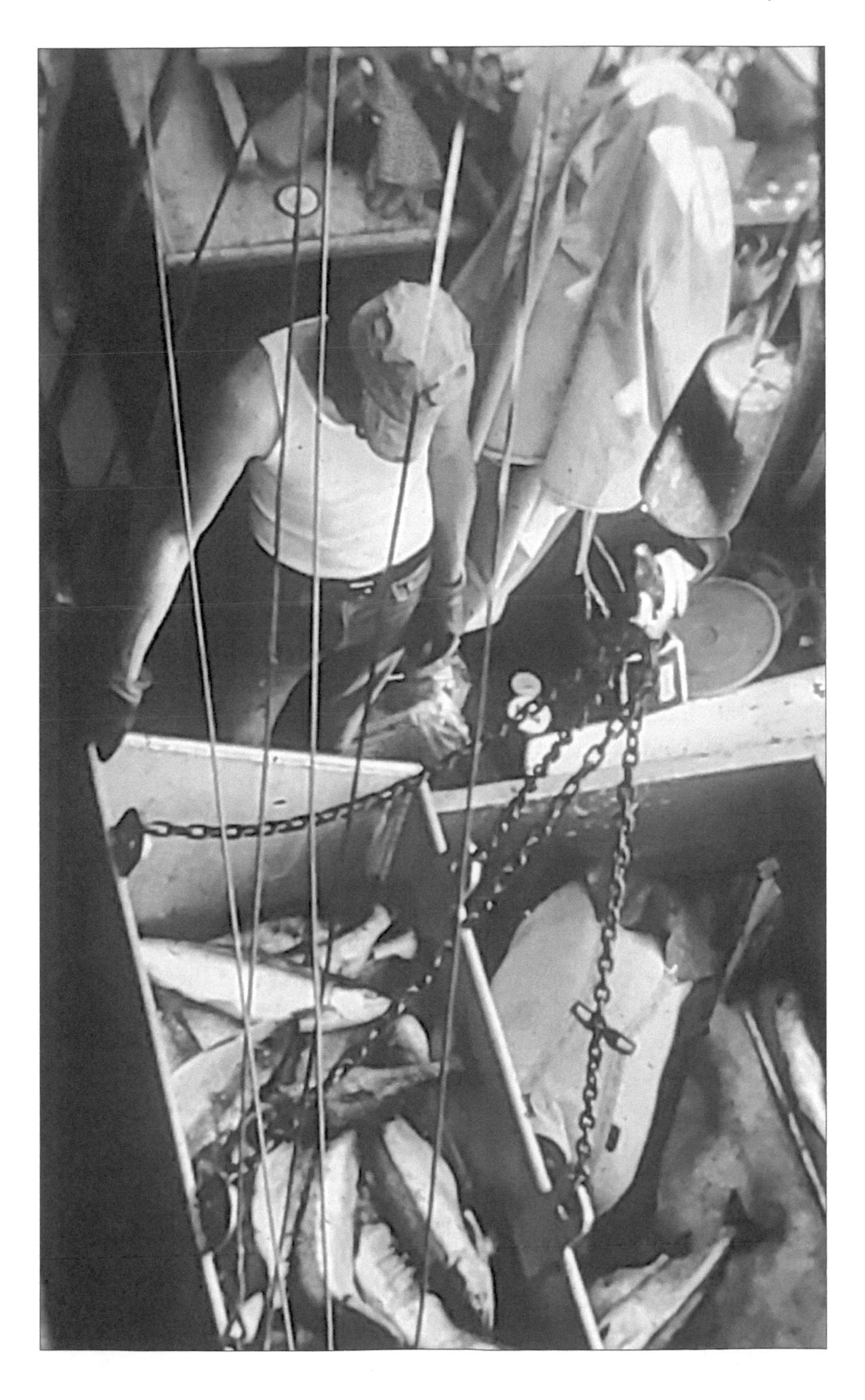

took one sniff and said I had time to go home and shower before returning. Ilse Christine Hill arrived on September 25, 1973.

It was during our second season that we ventured away from the Charlottes [Haida Gwaii]. We began as we did the previous year, fishing the west coast early and then trolling the east coast. We then put our new net on the drum and made the scary crossing of Hecate Strait to Prince Rupert. We fished for several weeks in Port Simpson [Lax Kw'alaams], where we tied up our boat on the net floats across from the village. A handful of women from the village came over daily to work on the nets there. It was from them that we learned how to mend our net.

The first time they came over, one of them approached me and asked, "What nationality are you... Vancouver?" They were wonderful ladies and we had great fun. In those days, there were hundreds of boats at each opening. Fishing at night, there were so many lights, boat lights and flashing lights on the end of each net. It was difficult once you picked up your net to find a new place to make a new set.

One week, we were high-boat fishing the Skeena. We picked what we thought was a good place to make our set. A gillnet is about 245-metres long and about 5-metres deep. We were sitting on the set noticing some of the floats sinking (signs of fish) when Rags came racing over in the *Roller Skate*.

"Nice looking set boys," he said, "but you better start picking it up. You'll be in the rocks over there in five minutes!"

Sure enough, we could see the strong current taking us onto the rocks. We started picking up quickly, watching the rapidly approaching rocks. Finally, we had to wind the fish in the net onto the drum. We got the last of the net into the boat just in time with Rags hanging by, laughing. We had to take the boat out into deep water and let the net out again to remove the fish, a nice set of sockeye. Beginners!

During the summer and fall of 1974, we travelled the entire coast from the Alaska border to Nanaimo. We spent three weeks in Milbanke Sound staying at a small company float. During off days, we canned salmon or took the net off and went out jigging ling cod, which we sold to our buyer. He had a small store that only carried two items: Kraft dinner and cases of Southern Comfort!

During that last season, we booked our fish with Babcock Fisheries. This means that we delivered to their buyers out at sea. They gave us a small percent as cash but at the end of the season they would pay the top dollar for the outstanding amount, which sounded good, except that Babcock Fisheries went bankrupt at the end of the season. My brother, Steve, went to a fancy office with a beautiful young receptionist in Vancouver.

There, he was told that we wouldn't get anything as we were not preferred creditors. Luckily, we had delivered to other buyers, some independent and some bigger like BC Packers, but we were still out at least 40 percent of our summer catch! While visiting Ucluelet that fall, we did see a former Babcock Fisheries office with a new name but the same people and a brand new truck sitting behind a chain-link fence. It was tempting…

We sold the *TRN 101* that fall in Nanaimo. I used my share to fund my first year at Simon Fraser University (SFU). I completed the professional development program in 1977 and began teaching. I returned to SFU in the early eighties and completed my prerequisite courses and then a dental degree in 1987 at the University of British Columbia. I practised dentistry on the coast for twenty-seven years. I went back to a number of the coastal communities as a locum dentist but those few years commercial fishing were some of the best times in my life!

U&I and *James Island*

Marvin Boyd

It was a perfect storm, a confluence of financial, legal and political matters that found me skipping across borders in the spring of 1971. I wasn't sure what I was looking for until I reached the Queen Charlotte Islands [Haida Gwaii]. The old saying, "Friends will get you through times of no money better than money will get you through times of no friends," became manifest when I met George and Donnette. I was living in a plastic teepee on the Tlell River and decided to hitchhike up to North Beach to spend a few days with my friend Dan Galloway, a.k.a. Dark Dan. He was living in an abandoned cabin on the beach and it was a lot more comfortable than a plastic teepee. George and Donnette picked me up, took me in and fed me until I got on my feet. They were caretaking a spread for Ted Bellis near Port Clements and we became friends for life.

When I began to meet people my age and see the freedom that they enjoyed, I started to understand the pressures that had driven me to that place and time. Strangely enough, I found it was exceedingly easy to be financially solvent as there were multiple employment opportunities. I could fulfill my inherited "Go West, young man" adventurous spirit: my

Marvin found the old saying, "Friends will get you through times of no money better than money will get you through times of no friends" to ring true in Haida Gwaii.

grandfather had taken a covered wagon out to the Oklahoma Territory and staked three hundred twenty acres of land for his honeymoon.

I became a warehouse man, logging truck driver and gas station mechanic, all in short order and with marginal success. However, I soon realized that, living on an archipelago of oceanic islands, I would need a boat to be able to see and appreciate it properly. A guy named Del Fowler had faith in me for some reason and I managed to procure a twenty-one-foot boat from him called the *U&I*. It had been built by Charlie Hartie in Queen Charlotte City [Daajing Giids] with help from Al Porter, who ran a small sawmill at the west end of town, and Al's right-hand man, Herb Saunders. I went to see Charlie, who was in the hospital at the time, and had a chat with him about the boat, where he had been and what he had wanted to do with it. I sent for my tools and proceeded to bring the boat up to speed mechanically, with some guidance from a local coastal pirate named Fred who lived on the dock.

The DFO paid Marvin to do what he loved best: cruise around on the *James Island*.

Being a flatlander from the Corn Belt of the Midwestern United States, I had no experience with the ocean. But in 1972, I set off in that boat for wild and amazing adventures in the South Moresby area. Very few people ventured that far south on the remote archipelago at that time, so the people I did meet in that area became instant friends and companions for life. I gave rides to and spent time with Bill Reid and Benita Sanders. I got to know local characters like Chief Dempsey Collinson, Joe Tulip and Percy Williams. If I had money for gas, I would be out there, cruising and learning about the history and appreciating the beauty of the area.

In 1973, I bought a thirty-four-foot boat called the *James Island* and found out that the Department of Fisheries and Oceans (DFO) would pay me for three to four months at a time to do what I liked most: cruising the area, walking creeks and counting returning salmon. I was ecstatic and stayed on that job for thirteen years, later becoming employed at the herring fishery as well. I worked on the mainland also, keeping track of returning sockeye and exploring new territory. I became friends with Jack Robinson, the captain of the *Arrow Post*, a DFO patrol boat. Jack came over to my boatshed on the beach in Charlotte and worked with me every day for three or four months re-planking and re-ribbing the *James Island.* We put on new decks and a new wheelhouse as well. When I put it back in the water, it was in good enough shape to stand up to the tough conditions on the coast. I asked Jack if he wanted to get paid but, in the end, I covered his lunch at Margaret's Café every day instead.

I had some float plane rides while working for the DFO. They flew us to town once in a ninety-day contract to do some shopping and banking, and I loved it. I later started an airplane charter business from scratch and ran it for twenty-two years out of Queen Charlotte City with my wife, accumulating over twelve thousand hours airtime flying Cessnas and Beavers on floats.

While living on the *James Island*, I became a diver and had all the latest equipment. I carried my compressor with me up and down the BC coast and did many dives on fishing boats, pulling nets and trolling wire from propellers. I became a geoduck diver on the west coast of Vancouver Island out of Tofino in 1979 and ran a boat called the *Marauder* for part of the fishing season there. I spent hours in the water every day harvesting huge clams for the Korean market. Also in 1979, I leased a boat called the *Kolberg*, grabbed a crew and went cash buying for herring on the BC coast. The price for herring skyrocketed and there were plane loads of cash being flown around and dropped off on boats. The company trusted me, I suppose because I had worked for so many years as a coastal patrolman. At one point, I had a cardboard box with half a million dollars in cash to distribute amongst the other cash buyers.

Crossing the Hecate Strait for a herring opening in the South Moresby area in a northwest gale, we got into a bit of trouble, snapped a stabilizer pole and took waves over the deck that filled up my speedboat with water. One of the crew climbed up the mast to unsnarl the rigging and we managed to get across in time, but the salt water contaminated the battery in the speedboat and it started spewing out a horrid green gas. I found out later the gas was deadly chlorine used in World War I, but we were lucky again and escaped without damage. There were three hundred boats in the area at that time and it rapidly became a big party with a bunch of crazy people on boats all tied together.

At Haida Gwaii and the North Coast, there was a community of like-minded people and we had many group dinners and social gatherings, after which we would pair up and go home. Life was good, full of love and adventure on the beautiful BC coast, and I truly enjoyed my forty-two years on Haida Gwaii.

U&I

Sam DiGregor

After graduating from Southern Illinois University in Carbondale, Illinois, in 1969, I spent the next two years trying to figure what the heck I was going to do with my life. As it happened, I found out that a biker buddy, Marvin Boyd, was living in a place called the Queen Charlotte Islands [Haida Gwaii]. At the time, I believed that humankind had evolved from the sea and that the ocean was the source of energy that created all life. I thought it would be a good idea to test that concept. Being an idealistic, enthusiastic twenty-five-year-old who was living in a quiet, low-key region of America's heartland, I realized that I needed to up the excitement factor in my life and go after new and challenging adventures. Horace Greeley said it well: "Go West, young man!"

Sam, eager to go after new and challenging adventures, followed Marvin to Haida Gwaii.

So began my vision quest. I got my act together and drove out to BC in 1972, travelling the coast and visiting numerous friends between Southern California to BC, looking for that special place to call home. The northern terminus of my quest was the Queen Charlotte Islands to visit Marvin and see if that might be the place for me to up my game. The day after I arrived, Marvin took me out to Marble Island and then down to South Moresby on the *U&I* (Charlie Hartie's old boat) for a few weeks that summer. I knew immediately that experience had set the hook deep.

Inspired by my adventures on the Charlottes, I spent the following winter and spring working for Twin City Barge and Towing out of Minneapolis, Minnesota, on the Mississippi River and on Lake Michigan hauling

Having grown up in Chicago, Sam knew little about boats before setting out on the *U&I*.

barges on tow boats. On one trip across Lake Michigan, in the fog, towing a fuel barge, I realized the captain hadn't turned on the radar and was lost. Since I had learned how to use the radar on the *Bonaventure* with Del Fowler the previous summer, I was able to show this captain from Arkansas how to use the radar. He had no idea. I think I bruised his ego though because he made things difficult for me after that, but disaster had been averted. I had saved the day.

I came back to BC the following spring as a landed immigrant. Before heading back to the Charlottes, I spent part of the early summer down in New Westminster helping Neil and Johnny McKinney rebuild their newly acquired but very old boat the *Kelpie*, which they planned to use to motor to the Islands that summer. I later heard that the boat gave it up around Salt Spring Island or thereabouts.

That summer, Marvin offered me the use of his boat, the *U&I*, while he was on a fisheries patrol charter. Of course, I didn't really know much about boats having grown up in Chicago, even with my summer travels and job on tugs. However, even though I didn't really know what I was doing, I was able to get the boat seaworthy and headed out to South Moresby for the summer. That trip was exciting, challenging and, once, nearly fatal, when Fred Watmough had to save my sorry bum from a sinking skiff. And the idea that I held space at a natural childbirth in the wilds of Burnaby Narrows totally blew my mind. What a learning curve!

In the summer of 1974, I fished salmon with Carl Coffey on the *Versatile* and between 1980 and 1986 I went herring gillnet fishing with him on the *Java Spirit*, travelling the coast from Mayne Island to Big Bay in some horrific weather.

Also during the eighties, my partner Marsha and I travelled to South Moresby in our fourteen-foot skiff for several weeks during the summers, living off the land: fishing, snorkelling and eating glasswort and other seaweeds. One year, a kid from a youth group visiting Hotspring Island [Gandll K'in Gwaay.yaay] took one of the oars from our skiff while we were in the pool. On our way back to Charlotte, our outboard quit near Sewell Inlet, so we had to use an axe and the other oar to paddle our way into the nearby logging camp, many hours later. The next day, I flew out to Charlotte with Trans-Provincial Airlines and returned with another motor. Another time, we even hitchhiked a ride on the *Arrow Post* with Captain Jack Robinson and crew to meet up with Marvin and Betsy on the *James Island* in Burnaby Narrows during fish patrol season.

From 1975 to 1984, I worked for the Department of Fisheries and Oceans (DFO) as a stream guardian in Rennell Sound, patrolling the streams from Cone Head to Clapp Basin while living in a four-metre trailer in Gregory Creek. In the beginning, I relied on the arrival of the Sooke post for weekly groceries as the road wasn't pushed through until sometime around 1980. Daily life involved cruising the area in a twelve-foot Springbok skiff, monitoring the logging company and counting salmon. I didn't own a big boat in those days, only a variety of skiffs and speedboats. My boating experiences were full of enormous joy, respect for the power of the sea and, at times, a certain amount of trepidation.

In 2005, I moved back to Southern Illinois for a variety of personal reasons and, after a seventeen-year hiatus, I am back in BC, living in Nanaimo. Marvin is still a close friend. Even though boats no longer play a significant role in my life these days, the memories of those days on the Charlottes vividly live on in my mind. There is no doubt that my time on the Charlottes played a pivotal role in my personal development in so many ways. How lucky I am.

Vanessa and *Sea Foam*

Gene Logan

When I graduated from high school in 1973, I couldn't get out of town fast enough. I had spent the last few years roaming the local mountains and hanging off rock walls in Squamish pretending to be a serious climber. I dreamt of building a log cabin in the wilds and using that as a base camp to access some really remote and beautiful backcountry.

I saved for a year, sold my Quad Electrostats and, along with a friend, chartered a helicopter to drop us and a bunch of supplies in the South Chilcotin wilderness. We built a log cabin the old way, with hand tools, and then headed back to Vancouver in the middle of December to rustle up funds for the next year's adventures. At the end of the following year, the drill was the same: try and find decent-paying work to keep this mountain man dream alive.

I enrolled in a basic seamanship course. The idea was to gain a position on a deep-sea freighter, work six months on the high seas and have six months to wander the headwaters of the Taseko Lakes, Chilko Lake, the Bridge River and Gun Creek. At the time, Canada's only merchant marine was in the Great Lakes and an industry-wide strike in the forests had shut down tugboating operations in BC, so my prospects weren't great. When I saw a notice of a deckhand course for trollers, I thought, *Why not? In for a penny, in for a pound.*

The course was great. We even got into a bit of bad weather off Point Atkinson when we went out to practise pulling the lines. I got recommended to the skipper of a troller and at the beginning of April we headed for the Queen Charlotte Islands [Haida Gwaii] via Prince Rupert.

Once we exited the big basin of the Georgia Strait and entered the passes and channels that lead to the tip of Vancouver Island, the air grew colder, the light dimmed and quiet settled over everything. Clouds cloaked the gradually diminishing mountains as the island curved north. At its end, we journeyed into the great, wide-open Queen Charlotte Sound, looking out at the way to Japan.

Crossing the sound required dropping the poles and employing the stabilizers. "Stabies" are weighted fins resembling an Avro Canada CF-105 Arrow that are dragged alongside the boat to slow the roll and make for a more comfortable and safer ride. We rode up and down enormous swells that rolled in from the west, smashing in giant white sprays along the mainland shore around Cape Caution. Caution was the order of the day, evident by the course of the Alaska ferry ahead of us, which was weaving through the sound. It took the swells either on the bow or the stern because to take them broadside would have caused mayhem on the car deck. Even with the minimum amount of rolling the ferry was doing, the car deck was still sure to be an insurance adjuster's nightmare.

Arriving in Prince Rupert was like stepping into a dream for Gene.

It is no coincidence that the sound is bookended by God's Pocket to the south and Safety Cove to the north. I was learning to respect any number of bodies of water: first Seymour Narrows earlier on the trip north, now Queen Charlotte Sound. Safety Cove is the start of the famous Inside Passage. As we continued north, it seemed like the cloud ceiling sank lower and lower until eventually it sat only a couple hundred metres above us. We passed Bella Bella, then Butedale, and as we entered Grenville Channel, it grew dark and I hit the bunk.

Arriving in Prince Rupert was like stepping into a dream. I had slept for the last leg and awoke at Cow Bay. The tide was low in a way I'd never seen before. The pilings of the dock stood nine metres over our heads and the ramp hung down at such an angle that you almost needed an ice axe and crampons to get up it. Sliding down the ramp was like flying down a ski course. We spent a week in Rupert and then it was off to the west coast of the Queen Charlottes to start fishing. And everything changed.

I thought I was tough from all the time spent building the cabin and hiking up mountains with a hundred pounds, but fishing was a different kind of tough. The hours were a shock: three or four hours of sleep a night if I was lucky and everything I did was too slow. My skipper was always yelling at me to speed up or do it another way. We weren't catching a lot of fish as it was early in the season, so I would take my time to do a good job dressing a fish. Often, I would lower the still-beating heart of a giant spring salmon gently into the water and release it while saying thank you. My skipper put an end to that, pushing me aside and showing me how he wanted me to dress fish. Slash. Rip. Fling. In a matter of seconds, the fish was dressed, the seagulls were fighting over the guts and his Helly Hansens were spattered with blood. I remember thinking, *Savage*.

I had had enough. I didn't dislike my skipper but I was tired of all the yelling and trying to function on no sleep. After three trips, we were back in Prince Rupert to deliver and I skidded down the ramp as I was wont to do and twisted my ankle. I was looking for an excuse to quit. I told him I wasn't going back out and immediately got on a seaplane and flew back to Masset. I never wanted to set foot on a commercial fishboat again.

In no time, I had a place to stay and a new circle of friends. This really was the best of times. I learned how to hunt octopus. I dug razor clams every big tide and learned how to smoke and can them. I hiked through the muskeg and journeyed out to the end of Rose Spit just to smell the flowers. I helped activist friends stop the southern part of Haida Gwaii from being logged barren and to fight a proposal to bring Exxon Valdez tankers into Kitimat. We had massage parties, dinner parties and benefit dances. We once hosted a buffet of local seafood for the American ambassador to hit home the true threat of an oil spill in local waters. Towards the end of August, though, I came up against the same wall that had chased me out of the mountains: I was broke. I flew back to Rupert and immediately got a cannery job and found a room in a house shared with folks I had met at environmental events in Masset. And… I met Lorrie.

Lorrie wanted badly to move across the harbour to Salt Lakes. People were squatting over there in vacation cabins that had long been abandoned. When the Americans built a highway to Prince Rupert during World War II, folks who had previously sought their recreation by boat exited Salt Lakes, bought cars and headed up the highway instead.

Eventually, we took over a cabin that was half built and became a part of the community. At the start, everything was new and a little bit scary. Paul Manson gave us a skiff: the *Vanessa* was a beamy fourteen-foot clinker that Paul had resurrected by fibreglassing the exterior. I bought a six-horsepower Evinrude outboard and a Husqvarna chainsaw and we were in business. The first time we crossed the harbour in a gale, we arrived back at Salt Lakes a little freaked out with the *Vanessa* half-full of water. Our neighbour simply said, "Didn't you bail?"

I had a job at a cannery working graveyard and quickly got used to commuting in all kinds of weather, day or night. I would beachcomb for firewood, roll a log off the beach, tow it home and tie it in front of the house to wait for the tide to recede. I always had a local tide chart in my

Gene stands on the bow of the *Breezeway* with his good friend Bill Smith, who talked him into having another go at fishing.

pocket and gradually became adept with a small boat. Sometimes, I would borrow a fast, light, little skiff. I would open the throttle, stand in the bow and steer by putting my weight on one side or the other. Other times I would row or put up a small spritsail that Lorrie made. Most of us never wore a personal flotation device of any kind.

There were also a lot of friends in Dodge Cove and Crippen Cove so there was always an excuse to jump in the skiff and go for a visit. Bill Smith, one of my best friends, had a small gillnetter with a B licence on it. A B licence was like an A salmon licence but with an expiry date. If the licence had only a year or two left, it was a cheap way to get into commercial fishing. Bill persuaded me to have another go at fishing and I was glad he did. Fishing meant more time on boats and I was in love with being on the water. Lorrie and I eventuality split up and I went south for the winter and then joined a friend who was trolling for a season in the Central Coast.

When I returned, Bill and I leased a boat together, although to be truthful, even though we shared everything down the middle (except dinner), it was Bill's show. He was the mentor and I was the mentee. The *Sea Foam* was a thirty-six-foot, double-ended wooden gillnetter. We had a fifty-fifty share agreement with the owner. We got a net and did okay. We were never highliners but seemed to catch enough to keep the owner happy. Along the way, we made a lot of mistakes, like getting the net in the wheel and falling asleep and running the boat aground.

When we got the net in the wheel (propeller), if we couldn't pull it out with the drum or chew it out with the prop, it meant someone had to dive down and cut it out. With no diving gear, we had to cut it free in three attempts or less. Any more and we would be too cold to make it out of the water.

As for falling asleep and hitting the beach, I have to take full credit for that. We were on our way south to Bella Bella for an opening after finishing a four-day opening in the Skeena. I stayed up yakking with Bill when I should have hit the bunk. When he couldn't keep his eyes open any longer, I took over. I lasted about an hour before I nodded off in the narrowest part of Grenville Channel. I awoke as we hit the beach with a loud *wham*, thinking, *I hope that's a log*. The tree branch in front of the wheelhouse windows told me otherwise.

The boat wasn't taking on any water and sat solidly on a small ledge. I shovelled out half our ice as the tide rose and when the wake of a seine boat lifted our stern we reversed off and headed back to Rupert. At the dock at Salt Lakes, I dove down to inspect the damage. One plank and the forefoot were slightly scuffed and splintered. I trimmed them smooth with a sharp hatchet and we went out for the opening in the Skeena. Because everyone had gone south, we ended up having a decent opening, doing much better than all the boats that went to Bella Bella. I was embarrassed about hitting the beach but the more I talked about it the more I heard, "I remember when I hit my first rock." As I found out, I was very lucky.

Worse mishaps involved heavy weather. Before Bill and I found the *Sea Foam*, we had taken out a forty-foot combination boat called the *Breezeway*. We went out for a shakedown cruise and did some trolling off Dundas Island outside Rupert. When the forecast called for a gale the next day, we decided to cross Hecate Strait right away and be able to fish in the lee of Graham Island.

About an hour into our crossing, it started to get dark and the wind that wasn't due for another twelve hours started to pick up. The seas built swiftly and before we knew it we were in the middle of a nasty gale in the middle of the top half of the strait. The top end is particularly nasty in a storm because of the shape of Hecate Strait, which is one-hundred-sixty-kilometres wide at the south end and only forty-eight kilometres across the top. Likewise, the bottom end is very deep but only ten fathoms at the top, which means when the tide and wind start pushing the water north it has only one place to go: up. The waves become huge, steep and breaking.

We were broadside to these waves and they were crashing into us relentlessly. The compass on the *Breezeway* had some major interference and was arcing about wildly. It was useless. We were trying to keep the bow a quarter into the waves but then risked running aground on Rose Spit, a long tongue of sand on the northeast corner of Graham Island that snakes out sixteen kilometres into Hecate Strait. The radar was of no use either. Somehow, we got in touch with a dragger who was to the north of us and in the lee of the island. He had us on his radar and dictated our course over the radio. At one point, a wave crashed over us and filled up the gillnet well. All our trolling gear was plugging the scuppers in the well and the stern was in danger of going under. I grabbed a twenty-litre pail, jumped into the stern and started bailing like mad as more waves crashed over the deck. I threw the trolling gear overboard and kept bailing. Eventually, I had it emptied and the self-bailers were able to do their job.

I had a floater vest and Bill had a floater jacket. These wouldn't save us but only meant that if we went over, our bodies would be found. I thought about tying the big, round boat bumpers called Scotchmen together to make a little raft in case we needed to abandon ship.

I don't get seasick as a rule but felt like I wanted to throw up. I tried repeatedly but nothing came up. I finally realized the knot in my stomach was fear. I gradually admitted to myself that I might die and after repeating that for a minute or two felt the knot loosen and my stomach ease. But, after another fifteen minutes of more waves hammering into us, I had to start the mantra all over again.

Bill would usually be sick as a dog but had taken some anti-seasickness pills and was doing okay. He held the helm the whole time with a white-knuckled grip. Every time a wave hit, water would somehow squirt around the window frames and drench him. I was on the radio with the dragger the whole time getting our directions. Otherwise, neither of us spoke.

After eight hours of this, we were finally in the lee of Rose Spit.

The wind was so strong though that even with a fetch of only about three nautical miles it was able to whip up a nasty, steep chop. Now, we were taking the waves almost head on. Every time we crested a wave, the plunge would kick up so much water that we were worried about blowing out the windows. Three hours later, we joined a small fleet of boats sheltering behind Tow Hill.

We weren't done yet. The *Breezeway* had a heavy, old, navy-style anchor that dragged three times before we were able to get it somewhat set. Each time it dragged, we had to pull it by hand as the winch wasn't working. On the fourth try, we set where there was no danger of drifting into another boat. We didn't care if we dragged all the way to Alaska. Even though we were completely exhausted, it took a while before the mix of nerves and adrenaline wore off and we were able to sleep. I liked being out in a good boat in rough weather, but this storm was worse than rough, it was ugly. It left me feeling overly cautious for some time after.

Years later, I would witness a hurricane off the west coast of Vancouver Island that claimed the lives of four friends: Rick, Pat, Thomas and Long John. Another year fishing halibut off the top end of Haida Gwaii, we had to run for Masset when the wind took a serious turn in strength. It took eight hours to cover what should have taken two. I remember we were heeled over so far that I was standing at the wheel with one foot on the floor and the other on the wheelhouse door. Six boats went down in

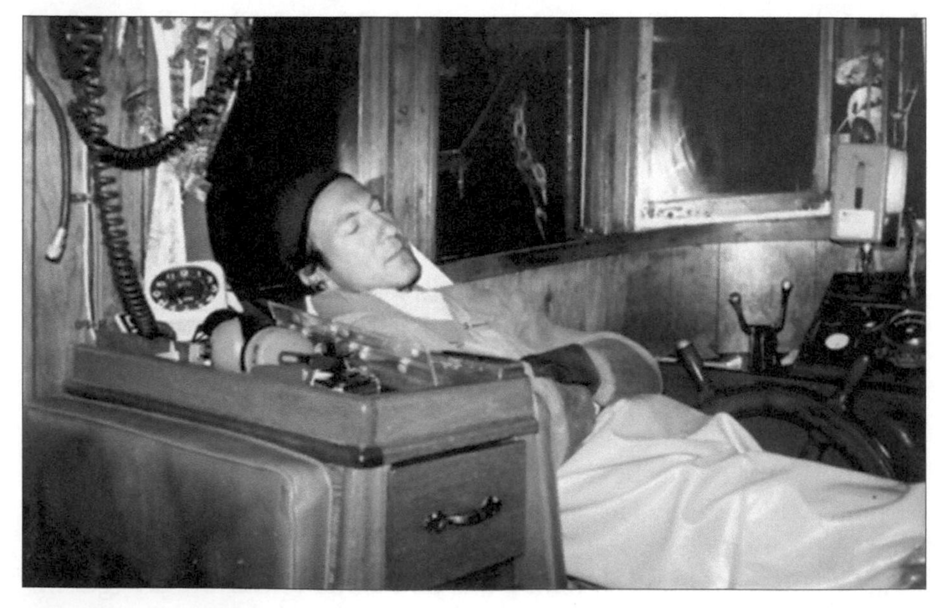

When Gene woke up to a tree branch in front of the wheelhouse windows, he knew he was in trouble.

Gene eventually moved on from fishing, when the opportunities became fewer and fewer.

that storm, one of them with a couple of friends on board. Fortunately, everyone was rescued from all the boats except one skipper.

I moved back to Vancouver in the mid-eighties and continued to fish until the late nineties. I stopped fishing when the opportunities became fewer and fewer and it became harder and harder to make a living. By then, fishing was second nature for me. I still felt that messing around on boats was just about the best thing a person could possibly do.

I feel privileged to have been in Prince Rupert in the seventies and taken part in what was essentially the last hurrah of commercial salmon fishing. I am still in awe of those amazing fish, how perfectly designed they are, how beautiful and how essential they are to this incredible coast. We will miss them dearly. As for the gang I first met in Prince Rupert, I don't miss them at all. They are all still my dearest friends.

Verna L

Gregg Best

Where it all began: my mother had a picture of me in a crib on the back of a gillnetter in Comox, where my dad was fishing with a boat called the *Gregory B.*

I was born in Victoria, went to school in Crofton and Chemainus, and graduated honours in engineering physics in 1973 from the University of British Columbia (UBC). I headed for the Queen Charlottes [Haida Gwaii] in a Ford F100 pickup with a homemade camper that summer. I bought a canoe in Masset, launched it in Moresby Camp and, with a friend, headed to Hotspring Island [G̲andll K'in Gwaay.yaay], stopping at all the Haida village sites along the way. We crossed Juan Perez Sound to Hutton Inlet and hiked up the creek, hoping to hike across Moresby Island to the west coast. Going was tough with lots of underbrush, so we had to quit and turn back. We paddled back to Moresby Camp, drove to Alliford Bay and took the Mitco barge to Skidegate Landing.

I started cutting firewood for sale, milling boards and timbers with my Alaska sawmill hooked to my Stihl 090 chainsaw, and cutting cedar shakes to roof houses on the island. I lived in Tlell for a while and hung out with people who were living there and on the beach in Naikoon Park and Cape Ball, eventually moving to Queen Charlotte City [Daajing Giids].

I went commercial halibut fishing around Langara Island as a deckhand on a small double-ender called the *Coney Isle* owned by Steve Atkins. We did okay. It seemed like we caught a halibut, ling cod or rockfish on every hook. That got me hooked, too, on fishing.

I met my wife, Anne, who worked at Margaret's Café and at the pub. Marg's Café was the local hangout. I went there for breakfast every day. If you got there before Marg, you had to make the coffee. There was no menu. Marg knew what everybody wanted. If she didn't like you, you didn't get anything. All the local characters were there. Buddy from Skidegate hitched in every morning to get there. He was always talking to himself out loud. Tourists didn't like it as he was saying awful things about people. If you listened closely, he was commenting about them. It didn't bother me. There was an old-timer, Sergius D'Bucy, who spotted the newcomers like me and challenged us: "So, you've come to build your empire here, eh?" Everybody in a small town knew everybody, what they said and what they did. I liked it, found that it kept people accountable and respon-

Born and raised on Vancouver Island, Gregg was accustomed to being on boats from a very young age.

sible. At Marg's, you could find work, you could get advice on how to fix things, you found out who to ask. I had a chainsaw and found people who needed firewood, so I got to work.

Eventually, I bought a thirty-seven-foot ex-troller called the *Verna L* from Barry Marks in Masset and took it to QCC. It needed a lot of work. My friend Ray Lagace helped me build a log cradle for it. Ray Pineault had an FMC track skidder that hauled it across the mud flat at low tide to the shore by Del Fowler's boatshed. We replaced planks and ribs and put a new cabin on with the help of Jack Robinson, who had a lot of shipbuilding knowledge. He was the skipper of the fisheries patrol vessel the *Arrow Post*. Toward the end of the refit, Harold Christiansen, local fisherman and boatbuilder, stopped by to see how we were doing and paid us the highest compliment when he said we could have done a lot worse! He looked around. He saw the place was a mess, projects and tools everywhere. I said it was not always like this. He disagreed. It was the nature of the business of building boats. Harold built the *Deena R*, a troller that fished out of Masset and was similar to the Wahl-designed fishboats elsewhere on the BC coast.

We did all right halibut fishing. We started on the west coast but the seas were too big and we eventually settled down fishing between Hotspring

Island and Cape Saint James, where we were the only local boat fishing halibut. Soon, due to my success, I had company. John Wier bought the *JMH* and the *Tomram*, Rick Nickerson bought the *Seal* and Keith (Flash) Rowsell bought the *Wanderbird*, and they were all converted to fish halibut. At that time, we fished about fourteen days at a time for five openings from May to September. We kept doing well, filling the *Verna L*, delivering to Mike Meegan at BC Packers in Skidegate Landing and to Prince Rupert.

Even though we had worked on the *Verna* to make it seaworthy, it was an old boat, built in the twenties. When we were crossing Hecate Strait delivering halibut to Prince Rupert, the bilge pumps could barely keep up with the water coming into the boat as the boat was now loaded past her old waterline. I didn't like it putting myself and crew at risk of sinking.

In 1986, we built a new boat we called the *Hopefull* (hope we're full) at the Gooldrup shipyard in Campbell River. Anne, my deckhand, Brian Pearson, his wife, Debbie, and I used ninety-five-by-one-hundred-seventy-litre barrels of fibreglass resin under the guidance of the shipyard. It took us twice as long and four times the original budget, but we eventually made the last halibut opening of that season. Interest rates went up to 15 percent that year so I went to work for the Department of Fisheries and Oceans (DFO) and ran a hatchery at Mathers Creek on Louise Island to get some

The crew did well on the *Verna L*, delivering to BC Packers in Skidegate Landing and to Prince Rupert.

winter income. I was also a roofer in Charlotte and built foundations for the school board's office. I did some handlogging in Dawson Inlet on the west coast. I ran the *CRC*, a classic old tug Ray and Derek bought in Prince Rupert. Ray and Derek had a permit to selectively log sections of the coastline. They fell the trees and limbed them and I ran the tug pulling the logs into the water. The slopes were steep and it was no easy job they performed, bucking fallen trees into sections and limbing. We boomed up the logs and after about a month we towed them through Skidegate Narrows to QCC. On the way, the boom got hung up on the east beacon for a couple of days, blocking the narrows until we freed it up.

A lot of fishermen lost their boats in the next year because of the interest rate increase but we managed to stay afloat. Halibut seasons got shorter as trollers started to fish halibut too. We started to fish spring salmon, chiefly out at Hippa Island on the west coast, and dabbled at fishing all around the Islands. We fished with our kids on board as soon as they were two years old. In the winter, we fished crab, starting with rings in Naden Harbour and then traps on the North Coast and Hecate Strait. Now, we were fishing twelve months a year. We bought another crab boat, the *Barbara K*, and had it for a while until I bought the *Nan Russ*, running crews three weeks on, three weeks off.

Boating along the Charlottes taught me to be self-reliant. I had to learn how to fix boats and learn how to respect the weather. There was nobody around to help if things went wrong. I had to have spares for anything that might break. I never had a breakdown where I needed towing or rescuing. Fishing crab in the winter in Hecate Strait taught me how to listen to forecasts and present weather conditions of wind and sea height. Often, we were the only boat out fishing. Typical southeast storms would switch to southwest, giving us a break to get at our crab gear.

But I got caught once. I was fishing about three hours south of Rose Spit. The weather forecast called for winds increasing to marginal gales. The wind started coming. In twenty-five to thirty knots, we could still fish. It started to increase even more. Soon they were calling for gales thirty-five to forty-five, so I stopped fishing and headed back toward Rose Spit. The seas were on the stern, so we were okay. Now, they were calling for storm-force winds. In the dark, we went around Rose Spit through the shortcut three kilometres off the Racon. (The Racon is a beacon that broadcasts its location to radar.) The doors and windows were closed and I was concentrating to make sure we kept the *Hopefull* from getting broadside to the waves, which were now breaking over the stern. Seas were over five metres. Wind now was close to one hundred knots. We rounded the spit and hugged

The *Verna L* was an old boat, built in the twenties.

the northern shore back to Masset. Wow. Close call.

Our kids were growing up so we decided to move to Comox, where they both graduated from high school and went on to UBC. Twenty years later, they both had the same physics professor as I had! Rebecca (named after a boat called the *Rebecca Lore*) got her PhD in environmental science and is now a professor at Northern Arizona University. When she was going to school in Charlotte, she was having trouble with math. My mom was visiting at that time and said, "Girls don't do very good at math." I would have none of that: I got some flash cards and fixed that. Rebecca relays that story to her first-year students every year! Lawren (named after Lawren Harris, a Group of Seven painter) got a bachelor of science in mechanical engineering (boat design) and is now a partner at Robert Allan Ltd. in Vancouver, which designs oceangoing tugs for worldwide use.

I sold my boats on the Charlottes, both the *Nan Russ* and the *Hopefull*. I bought a couple of crab/prawn boats (the *Tsunami* and the *Golden Penny*) and fished out of Tofino, Sooke and eventually out of Cowichan Bay. I built three aluminum prawn boats, the *Silver Swift*, the *Quicksilver Girl* and the *Charisma*. We bought a small seafood shop in Cowichan Bay and each year held a prawn festival there till we relocated to Victoria, where we are now. We own a retail and take-out fish market in Oak Bay and a seafood processing and distribution facility (Better Seafood Supply) in Saanich, serving Victoria restaurants and retail grocery stores.

I was twenty-three when I moved to the Haida Gwaii, thirty-five when I left. I am grateful to so many friends who helped and supported me in those years and, of course, to my wife, Anne, who supported me in all my life's projects. I have no boats now. Boats shaped my life and my family.

Wanderbird

Keith Rowsell

In 1975, my wife, Barb, our four-year-old son, Joshua, and I lived in a floathouse at the south end of Nitinat Lake on the west coast of Vancouver Island. Nitinat Lake is accessed by fifty-six kilometres of logging road from Cowichan Lake, then twenty-two kilometres by water. Boats were a big part of life. Aside from travel by boat, we were log salvaging and crab fishing. We bush-milled fir and cedar planks to build a roomy scow for the crab fishing, my first boatbuilding effort. It worked out well.

One day, a smooth talker named Rudy Kovach came and asked if we would like to move to the Charlottes [Haida Gwaii] and mill wood for a longhouse for the Skidegate Band Council. We had just milled six tonnes of big cedar planks for him for an exhibit in the museum in Ottawa. I met Rudy in Vancouver in the spring and flew to Sandspit. That flight changed my life: the endless snow-covered mountains, long inlets, sprinkles of islands. My first thought after my first sight of the Charlottes was, *We will need a bigger boat*. We packed everything up to ship on the *Northland Prince* ferry and made the move.

The milling job went well. We bought a little house up coast and settled in. The Islands were busy, with logging and fishing going full speed before environmental concerns. We met incredible young people who were building floathouses, cabins in the bush and on Hippy Hill, taking derelict boats off the beach and rebuilding them. One boat had the top of a VW van as a wheelhouse. Creativity was rampant: carvers, painters, spinners, weavers, knitters, writers, actors (good and bad), woodworkers, you name it.

Keith and his family lived on a floathouse on Nitinat lake before moving to Haida Gwaii.

Our search for a boat was disappointing. I started working for Dick Vernon, who was putting together a shop to service the logging and fishing industries. I was to do the woodwork and he would do the welding, machining and mechanical work. One day, I had finished fibreglassing the hatch for a troller but it was too early to go home. Dick had cut the plate for a set of fuel tanks for the troller. He went off, so I welded, pressure tested and painted the tanks, then went home. The next day, Dick demanded to know who had finished the tanks.

When I told him that I had, he said, "Bullshit, you're fired. I want to hire the guy who welded these tanks."

I started packing up and his wife came into the shop and asked what all the yelling was about. When Dick told her, she answered that she had seen me do it. I showed Dick the tickets from my apprenticeship in Ontario and he apologized. He hired me back, but I told him it had to be at a welder's pay rate.

The fishing industry was booming. Gas engines were going out and new diesels were going into the boats, along with steel engine beds, exhausts, endless brackets, hydraulics, pumps, alternators, generators, refrigeration units and compressors. There was a demand for welding in aluminum, so Dick bought an aluminum gun and we learned to use it as the fleet changed to aluminum trolling poles, brackets and drums. As the fleet modernized so did the logging equipment, which started to take over the business and took me further from boats.

The *Wanderbird*, originally built in 1946 by Jack Cummins, needed a bit of work by the time Keith and Barb bought it in 1979.

Barb and I had met Gregg and Anne Best, who fished halibut on the *Verna L.* Their stories of fishing intrigued us. The hard work they put into their boat was impressive. We had been looking at sailboats when an old, Wahl-built wooden gillnetter that had been on the beach for a couple of years came up for sale. We had it towed to below the tide line and waited, our anxiety rising with the ocean. We had buckets and a gas pump. Barb and I went over all the seams, caulked where needed, trying to match the old tension so no hard spots prevented the seams from seating evenly, puttied seams and nail heads, and painted the bottom. As the tide rose, we bailed with the buckets. By the time the boat was afloat it looked like a sprinkler, but the buckets were keeping up. We towed the boat to the dock and spent the night bailing, but by morning the incoming water had slowed to a dribble. Several locals had previously owned the boat, so lots of people stopped by with stories and encouragement. Eventually, the owners came by and said now that it was looking so good they wanted more money. So, we packed up and walked away. Eventually, it was towed back to the beach and about a year later they burned it. We were a little sad but it made us more determined.

We bought the *Wanderbird* in 1979. It was designed and built in 1946 by Jack Cummins, who lived in Knight Inlet. It was yellow-cedar planked on oak frames, powered by the original Cummins diesel, thirty years old and tired. It was fishing halibut out of Rupert at the time. Ray Lagace bought the tug the *CRC* at the same time, so we crossed the Hecate Strait together. The *Wanderbird* had radar so we were in the lead. Halfway across, the engine quit and I couldn't get it to start again, so Ray passed us a tow line. Then we ran into fog, so I fired up the radar to keep us on track. Next day, I charged the batteries, took the pump apart, couldn't find anything wrong, put it back together and started it up. It ran fine. (Six months later in a logging camp, an old mechanic told me that when an engine quits, you take it apart, swear at it, put it back together and it might work for years or quit the next day.)

That first fishing season was a disaster. Nothing was properly set up, setting out gear was dangerous, picking it up was worse, most of the ground line that came with the boat was rotten. Somehow, though, with no rhyme or reason, we caught enough fish to make the payment and pay the crew. I went back welding to pay for fuel, bait, electronics and gear. Halibut was an early season fishery, so trolling, gillnetting and seining were just starting. As I worked on different boats, I asked endless questions. On the *Wanderbird*, I built an aluminum chute and bait trays, hook racks, railings around the stern and pipe hoops over the stern for the skiff and to keep some of the rain off the crew when setting gear. I extended the railings along the port side for safety and to hang anchors, flags and a swing boom for hauling the ground line.

In those days, fishing families came down to clean and prepare the boats. Women cleaned the inside (stove, pots, pans and every surface was scrubbed) and the men scraped and painted the engine room, hull and decks. It was a wonderful time, with kids running around, fishing and playing; elders telling stories of the old days; pickup trucks arriving full of gear that people packed down the docks in wheelbarrows and on their backs. No empty hands went back or forth. On the way up the dock, we asked, "Is this going to your truck?" Joking was constant; someone would yell out, "Hey, you missed a spot." Whenever a paintbrush would stop, every painter would look, then the laughter and swearing would start. Good memories.

The *Wanderbird* needed some deck planks and part of the starboard bulwarks replaced. Those areas get lots of abuse. Piles of red and yellow cedar were packed down to the dock to replace the rotten planks. I like to gather all materials and prep first, so I started hand planing the covering boards, spreading shavings all over the dock.

Along came a Haida lady and she started in on the mess I was making. "Clean this up, people need to walk through here," she said and she stomped off. The laughter and clapping started; everybody around loved the show. I got the hint and cleaned up.

The next day she stopped, looked around, looked the boat over, nodded and said, "Don't paint the inside of the cabin white, especially around the windows. It ruins your night vision," and walked off.

Godfrey and Mabel were good friends; their boat was a beautiful Wahl double-ender called the *Island Bay*. They loved to see us young people on the docks. One day, Godfrey saw me planing four-by-fours and asked what I was building, so I told him my plans for the bulwarks.

He said, "Oh, that sounds great. I was never good at woodwork, but my brother works in Rupert at the shipyard. He's good at this kind of thing." He then started to tell me stories about boats that his brother rebuilt, how he built covering boards and sistered ribs, how he dealt with rotten rib ends, how he caulked the seam against the deck lightly and against the planking, and how he mixed linseed oil and white lead for seams around ribs and tapped cedar wedges in. As Godfrey told me more about his brother, it became clear he was actually telling me how to do it properly. With a smile, he said, "Well, see you tomorrow." After he left, I took everything apart and started again.

The *Wanderbird*. In 1981, Keith and his family were thrilled to secure a four month contract with fisheries.

In 1981, we decided to get out of fishing. We sold the licence, which reduced our debt. Interest rates were over 20 percent at that time. We still needed to earn a living and were scratching our heads when one of the local fisheries officers came down and asked if we would be interested in a one-hundred-twenty-four-day contract on the west coast. That sounded like heaven. We scrambled to get ready, stripping all the fishing gear and taking it home to store, loading in a new oil stove, packing our personal gear and renting out our house. Next morning, Barb shopped, we fuelled up, loaded up everything, including our two sons, at that time ten years and five months old, and headed for Skidegate Narrows. We just made the tide, ran down to Englefield Bay, dropped the anchor and passed out. Next morning, as we entered Tasu Sound, we saw a glass ball floating in front of us and we took it as a good sign. The next four months were spent walking streams, counting salmon, cruising to locate schools of returning salmon and generally enjoying the inlets and beaches of the west coast. We spent most of our time in Tasu Sound, where we got to use the facilities of the mining community: a great recreation centre with a swimming pool, showers, sauna and a good, little grocery store. They had pizza night on Fridays and would deliver to the boat at the dock if we happened to be there. We got to meet some very nice people who worked and lived there.

In late August 1982, storm warnings from the northwest were predicted, so we headed up to Newcombe Inlet to tie up for the night. Newcombe is sheltered from the northwest, but during the night the wind changed to southeast and it pushed us against the log float. By the time we got free, the boat was damaged. We were taking on water but the pumps kept up. It was blowing thirty-five, gusting forty, a nasty night. We ran south to Fairfax Inlet and tied up as the sun came up. On the port side, we found two metres of seam missing between two planks below the waterline. We moved everything on board to starboard, but that was still not enough, so we hung the skiff from the stabilizer pole and filled it with water. The seam just cleared the water. I caulked it with cotton and then filled it with cement. The temporary fix enabled us to finish the rest of the season with no problems.

We were having so much fun on the boat we spent much of the winter in Rose Harbour. The anemometer at the Cape Saint James lighthouse only goes to one-hundred-three knots, but the lightkeepers figured that one storm gusted to one-hundred-eight knots. That was pretty exciting. Back in Queen Charlotte City [Daajing Giids] in early spring, we put the *Wanderbird* on the beach to re-caulk the bottom. We pulled out all the caulking below the water line. One butt seam was hard to clean out, so I got my hook tool and started digging when all of a sudden, the plank popped off and fell on the ground. Then we really thought about all the rough weather. We re-nailed the hull up to the guard rails, re-caulked and payed the seams, and then painted the whole side, a very careful and conscientious job. We had the *Wanderbird* for another eight years. After our experience with scary planks, even though the bottom was now in good shape, it was still an old wooden boat.

In Rose Harbour, we thought that when you live on a boat you feel you own whichever inlet you are in and if you don't like the neighbours, you just up anchor and head out. In 1984, we started to build the *Anvil Cove*, a fifty-three-foot steel schooner, on Hippy Hill in Queen Charlotte. It took us six years. After launching the *Anvil Cove* in 1990, we had the best life possible, working for twenty-five years in the charter business. While we mostly did mothership kayaking tours, we also took out a lot of researchers: the Canadian Wildlife Service for seabird studies, Parks Canada archaeologists, National Geographic and surveyors of peregrine falcon populations. We met many very interesting people from all over the world and all walks of life.

I have continued building aluminum boats. Everything from ten footers to thirty footers, about twelve in all. Most were built from scratch but a few were re-built herring punts, one for Parks Canada with integral fuel tanks to be their fuel barge for the Gwaii Haanas National Park Reserve.

Haida Gwaii was visited by more than just eager fishermen—the Canadian Wildlife Service and National Geographic came to study birds and sealife.

Some boats were for researchers but most were for local people to fish and explore the waters of Haida Gwaii. I'm now just finishing a seventeen footer, the fifth of a series that I designed. This will be for us to put out our crab pots, beachcomb, fish and just get out on the water. We currently have a thirty-five-foot fibreglass cruiser that we don't get out on enough.

Barb and I worked side by side on all our adventures. Every morning at breakfast, we look out at Skidegate Inlet, watch the sun come up and tell ourselves how fortunate we are, now and during our life on the water.

In 2014, Barb and I drove across the country to Newfoundland to discover my family's shipbuilding history. My great-grandfather built the last three-masted schooner built in Newfoundland. It seems the circle is complete.

York, *Kanu* and *Bokay*

Steven Clark, a.k.a. Beaver

In the early spring of 1970, I hitchhiked to Prince Rupert and stood in line for work at the Canadian Fishing Company plant, where I memorized the sign. It read, "Sammy Seal Seaside Super Selective Sockeye Salmon Suction System." I didn't get that job, but I did get a job at Booth Fisheries, at the Royal fish plant. I was seventeen years old.

My first boat was a thirty-foot double-ender, the *York*. I fished crabs, clams, abalone, cod and halibut. During those days, you could fish everything with one licence.

I spent lots of time living in my boat, exploring little places on the North Coast such as Georgetown, Big Bay and Billy Bay on Porcher Island with Cow Bay being the main tie up.

I sold the *York* to a woman named Darcy. I was planning to go back to Clearwater, where I had spent some time before I lived in Rupert. However, during the same time, I met my life partner, Francine, a Gumboot Girl, so I decided to return. There was now an attraction in Rupert.

In those early years of my fishing career, I got a lot of help and fishing advice from Percy Green and his two sons, Henry and Herby, three Indigenous people from Lax Kw'alaams. Our friendship with them led to Francine managing the seasonal fish camp at Goose Bay on Dundas Island for Mrs. Klassen (the owner, who lived in Lax Kw'alaams) and BC Packers (which processed the fish delivered to the camp). We had a long connection with Lax Kw'alaams, also known as Port Simpson, and its people.

My second boat was a salvage boat from the Rivtow yard situated on the waterfront just beside the old elevator. It was a forty-foot double-ender renamed the *Kanu*—a long and narrow boat that cut through the waves like a knife but when you travelled sideways, it was chucking (pucking) all the way. Francine and I worked long hours re-planking, re-corking, changing the engine and painting.

On the *York*, everything was done by hand. Hauling seven skates of longline by hand was crazy but we were young and a bit ignorant and we did it. As Alf Carlson, the captain of the packer the *Colnet*, used to say, "We were so strong we had muscles in our shit."

The *Colnet* was the packer that delivered everything to the Goose Bay, Canoe Pass and TW3 fish camps, a service of the past. They served mostly Indigenous people and the fishermen who did not want to ice their fish. This was before boats had freezers. And Alf could tell you the history of everything and everyone in the dialect of the day, inappropriately colourful.

Stephen lived on his boat, exploring little spots along the North Coast.

On the *Kanu*, we installed a longline drum, hydraulics and even a saltwater pump. After almost getting run over by the Alaska ferry while in the fog off Dundas Island, we added a radar. We were getting a little wiser and we were learning the trade, always trying to fish hook and line for halibut, black cod, ling cod and rock fish.

Over time, the fishing industry went through some fundamental changes. I was not in favour of the quota system and the separation of every species into individual licences and quotas. I believe that policy ended the small fisherman that made up those small communities and, in my opinion, did not serve conservation, sustainability or Indigenous concerns.

To survive the changes and continue to fish for a career, I bought a salmon boat named the *Bokay*. That was the beginning of our trolling life. At the time, we lived in Oona River on Porcher Island. I really learned a lot living there. We liked it but Francine felt it was too far out, a two-and-a-half-hour boat ride from Prince Rupert. After two years of living there with our two girls, we decided to move closer to town and bought a house in Dodge Cove on Digby Island. At the time, Dodge Cove hosted a few fishermen like me, not born into it but ready to give it a try.

Special thanks are due to John Leakey, a long-time friend, who was working at the old grain elevator at the time. He took an interest in me, a real rookie trying to curve a plank without breaking it. His help was invaluable and served me well, as all my boats needed constant work to stay afloat. Iver Wahl, from the well-known boatbuilding Wahl family, called me a master of haywire when I bought the *Bokay*. You got that right, Iver. Some might call me the King of Crap but you need to be crafty to work with old boats.

I never took the family longlining, but salmon fishing along the top end of the Queen Charlotte Islands, now known as Haida Gwaii, was a family affair. Masset Inlet, 7 Mile Point [Mia Kun], Naden Harbour, Pillar Bay, the Circle Jerk and the waters off Langara Island were our safe trolling spots with our two children, who spent many summers on the back of the *Bokay* learning to differentiate the different salmons. We came to know other families with kids who grew up on the back of fishboats. It made a special community of fishers.

When I bought the *Bokay*, it came with a gillnet for the fall chum salmon fishery. On the first gillnet trip in the Boston Rocks area, with the help of Captain Barb Howe, I caught big sockeyes and lots of early chums and made lots of money. But it didn't take long to lose half the net in the Nass River area on the second gillnet trip. Damn tide rips and logs!

After that was a fall fishery opportunity that extended the salmon season. My friend Des Nobels on the *Vondie D* lent me a net for a sockeye opening but it turned out it wasn't his net. Oops! It was blowing a heavy westerly and, being a fair-weather troller, I could not take the rough seas on the west side of Stephens Island, so I took refuge in a safe bay. I saw all these jumpers around the boat, so I threw the net out and got hundreds of sockeyes. Thanks, Des!

Kanu was a salvage boat, and Steven and Francine worked long hours re-planking, re-corking, changing the engine and painting to get the boat back in shape.

During the last year that we could fish the whole coast, we fished chum salmon all the way down the coast: Spiller Channel, the Bella Bella area, Port Hardy, Winter Harbour, Nootka Sound, Nitinat Lake and finally Qualicum.

Sadly, in October 1984, we lost good people who were fishing in the Nootka Sound area to the remains of a tropical hurricane. It came so quick that even the marine weather channel did not report it early enough for some fishermen to find anchorage in time. Long John Secord, Thomas, Rick and Pat died during that storm. I don't forget the fishermen that have gone before, and there have been many, too many for this short story.

Trolling the top end of Haida Gwaii became our family summer workcation. Francine, our two daughters and I fished spring salmon and coho. We went to the beach and found glass balls, whale bones and strange treasures. We anchored in every safe harbour from 7 Mile Point to Tasu, some not so safe. Wind, waves, whales and fish!

Sadly, that lifestyle is just a shadow of what it was. Gone are the canneries, small boat shops and sawmills. Almost all the kids leave the small island communities. That circle has broken. We, too, decided to sell our boat and licences and relocate.

We were lucky to have lived at a time of plenty of fish, friends and families. A way of life mostly gone but not forgotten. It seems our kids keep a bit in touch with other fisher kids. That must be our legacy.

Glossary of Selected Nautical, Fishing and Forestry Terms

anemometer: an instrument for measuring the force of the wind
autopilot: a system used to control the path of a vessel without requiring constant manual control by a human operator
baggywrinkle: a soft covering for cables (or any other obstructions) to reduce sail chafe
bulkhead: an upright partition separating the compartments in a ship
daggerboard: a kind of centreboard which slides vertically through the keel of a sailing boat
deckhand: a person employed on a ship's deck, sometimes taking wheel watches
dog: a toggle with a line driven into a floating log in order to tow it
dory: a small flat-bottomed fishing boat with high sides
double-ender: a boat in which stern and bow are tapered
dragger: a fishing boat equipped with dragnets; a trawler
faller: a logger who cuts down trees
ferro-cement: a system of construction using cement reinforced with steel
flywheel: a heavy wheel on a revolving shaft used to regulate machinery or accumulate power
fo'c'sle: slang for "forecastle," the forward part of a ship where the crew has quarters
freeboard: the part of a ship's side between the waterline and the deck
gaff: a stick with an iron hook for landing large fish or a spar to which the head of a fore-and-aft sail is bent
geoduck: a giant mud-burrowing bivalve mollusc
gig: a light ship's boat for rowing or sailing, or a rowboat, especially for racing
gillnet: a net suspended vertically to entangle fish by the gills
gunwale: the upper edge of the side of a boat or ship
gurdy: a winch on a fishing boat used to haul in a line, net, etc.
gyppo: a minor or small-time logging operator or contractor
handlogger: a person who logs by hand, using tools such as an axe or saw, sometimes jacks and pulls the logs into the water with a boat

herring punt: a broad, flat-bottomed, open, usually aluminum boat with a low freeboard, used for herring fishing
herring roe: the yellowish eggs of pregnant herring on their way to spawn, eaten as a food and considered a delicacy
highliner: a successful fisherman who catches significant numbers of fish
in-breaker: a worker in their first season in the fishing industry
keel: the lengthwise timber or steel structure along the base of a ship
keelson: a line of timber fastening a ship's floor timbers to its keel
ketch: a two-masted fore-and-aft rigged sailing boat with a mizzen-mast located forward of the rudder and smaller than its foremast
lapstrake: a clinker-built boat
log boom: a barrier of floating timber to contain, restrain or guide floating logs
longline: a deep-sea fishing line with a large number of baited hooks attached to it
longshoreman: a person employed to load and unload ships
pram: a small utility dinghy with a transom bow rather than a pointed bow
punt: a long narrow flat-bottomed boat, square at both ends, used mainly for pleasure on rivers and propelled by a long pole
schooner: a fore-and-aft rigged ship with two or more masts, the foremast being smaller than the other masts
scow: a flat-bottomed boat used as a barge
scupper: a hole in a ship's side to carry off water from the deck
seine: a fishing net for encircling fish, with floats at the top and weights at the bottom edge, attached ashore at one end
skidder: a type of powerful four-wheel tractor used to haul logs from a cutting area
skiff: any of various types of small light boat, esp. one adapted for rowing and sailing
sloop: a small, one-masted, fore-and-aft-rigged vessel with mainsail and jib
stabilizer: a gyroscopic device to prevent rolling of a ship
trawler: a boat used for fishing with a trawl line or seine
trimaran: a sailing vessel similar to a catamaran, with three hulls side by side
troller: a boat used for fishing by dragging bait along in the water behind a moving boat
williwaw: a sudden violent squall blowing offshore from a mountainous coast

About the Editors

Lou Allison moved to the West Coast from Ottawa in the western migration of the 1970s. She settled in Dodge Cove after having children, working all over the North Coast, and living on boats and float houses with her partner, Jeremiah, while completing her English degree by the light of a kerosene lamp. Lou now works full time at the Prince Rupert Library and is devoted to all things related to books. She is the editor of the bestselling anthologies *Gumboot Girls* (2012) and *Dancing in Gumboots* (Caitlin Press, 2018), with Jane Wilde. With *Gumboot Guys,* Lou looks forward to another opportunity to read and share the stories of our North Coast lives.

Jane Wilde moved to the West Coast in the early 1970s from Guelph, Ontario. She resided on Haida Gwaii from 1976–79 and, after attending nursing school, returned to Prince Rupert as a maternity nurse. For thirty-five years, Jane worked in health care in rural communities, living in Dodge Cove and Prince Rupert with her partner, Richard. She relocated to the Comox Valley in the fall of 2016. She compiled stories and images for the bestselling anthologies *Gumboot Girls* (2012), *Dancing in Gumboots* (Caitlin Press, 2018), and *Gumboot Guys* (Caitlin Press, 2023), with editor Lou Allison.

Acknowledgements

We would like to thank the writers who shared their stories: for many, the exercise of writing was a real stretch and they really came through! Thanks are also due to our publisher, Vici Johnstone and her stellar staff at Caitlin Press, who continue to support and encourage us; our friends and families who patiently bear with us as we obsess over all the details; and our generous readers for their collective enthusiasm. Lou would also like to thank, once again, her kind and supportive colleagues at the Prince Rupert Public Library.